Materials Science
AIR

making use of the secrets of matter

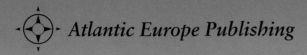
Atlantic Europe Publishing

First published in 2003 by
Atlantic Europe Publishing Company Ltd.

Author
Brian Knapp, BSc, PhD

Art Director
Duncan McCrae, BSc

Senior Designer
Adele Humphries, BA, PGCE

Editors
Mary Sanders, BSc, and Gillian Gatehouse

Illustrations
All by David Woodroffe, except David Hardy 20-21

Design and production
EARTHSCAPE EDITIONS

Scanning and retouching
Global Graphics sro, Czech Republic

Print
LEGO SpA, Italy

Materials Science – Volume 9: Air
A CIP record for this book is available from the British Library

ISBN 1 86214 323 4

Acknowledgments
The publishers would like to thank the following for their kind
help and advice: *Bedassa Jote Gobena*; *Brother Industries Ltd
(Japan)*; *Liz Clough*; *Jonathan Frankel*; *Tim Fulford*.

Picture credits
All photographs are from the Earthscape Editions photolibrary
except the following: (c=center t=top b=bottom l=left r=right)

Brother Industries Ltd (Japan) 30b; *Chubb Security Group* 50;
Corbis 23t; *Mary Evans Picture Library* 11tr; *NASA* 18-19,
44-45, 51; *The Stock Market* 9bl, 37br; *USGS* 47tl (Austin Post).

*This product is manufactured from sustainable managed forests.
For every tree cut down, at least one more is planted.*

Contents

(*Left*) Clouds contain the same range of molecules as clear air, except that the water vapor molecules have changed to liquid water droplets.

1: Introduction

A MATERIAL is something that people work with to make something that others need. Anything that is SOLID, LIQUID, or GAS can be a material. This book is about the most common MIXTURE of gases—air.

Air is all around us, and it has enormous uses, although mostly we are not aware of them. This book tells how we use air and the things in it. But to see how we use gases like air, we must first look into the curious world of gases and how they behave.

(Above) For thousands of years many people believed that the materials from which everything else was made were air, fire, earth, and water, known at that time as the elements. Of them none is any longer regarded as a true chemical ELEMENT, although the air is known now to contain mostly a mixture of elemental gases.

How gases were discovered

It so happens that solids and liquids, which are the easiest to handle, have complicated structures and properties, while gases, which are the hardest to handle, have the simplest properties.

The difficulty of handling gases was an enormous handicap to the first people studying materials, and it actually held back the understanding of materials for centuries. Because the first chemists worked with solids and liquids (the most complicated materials) instead of the simplest (gases), they found it very difficult to develop theories of matter.

But this did not mean that people were not interested in the way that gases could help them overcome some serious problems. It simply meant that they used gases without understanding what they were made from.

One example of the use of air came about through the need to mine coal from deep shafts. These shafts readily filled with water and so were prone to flooding. As a result, some means of pumping out the mines was extremely important.

The solution proved to be the suction pump. However, although the pump worked, it was not then understood that it was because the air all around us is under PRESSURE. After all, we do not feel the pressure of the air on our bodies. But that is because we have air at the same pressure inside us as exists around us. The pressure of the air only becomes apparent if the pressure is lowered in a container—as it is in a suction pump.

(Left) When you suck on a straw, you reduce the pressure of the air on the liquid in the straw, and that causes an imbalance of pressure. The pressure of air on the liquid in the glass is now greater than the pressure on the liquid in the straw, and so air pressure forces liquid up the straw.

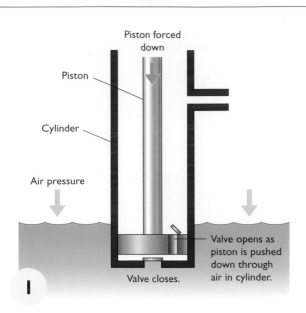

Piston forced down

Piston

Cylinder

Air pressure

Valve opens as piston is pushed down through air in cylinder.

Valve closes.

1

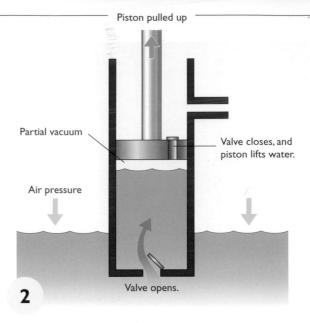

Piston pulled up

Partial vacuum

Valve closes, and piston lifts water.

Air pressure

Valve opens.

2

(Above) This diagram shows the principle of the suction pump. A tightly fitting piston is moved up and down a cylinder that is partly submerged. There are one-way valves in the bottom of the cylinder and in the piston. On the downward stroke the valve in the piston opens and allows air out (1). On the upward stroke a partial vacuum occurs in the cylinder, and the valve is pushed open by the water, which then flows in (2). On the next downward stroke the cylinder valve shuts, and the piston valve opens, allowing water to move into the space above the piston (3). On the next upward stroke water is drawn into the cylinder at the bottom and at the same time is ejected from above the piston (4).

In a suction pump a cylinder is fitted with a piston, and the lower end of the cylinder is placed in water. When the piston is raised in the cylinder, it increases the volume of space below the piston. The air that was originally in this space at atmospheric pressure is now at a very low pressure because the volume it can fill has been made larger by pulling up the piston.

As a result, the air pressure inside and outside the cylinder are unbalanced. Because the atmospheric pressure is greater than the pressure in the cylinder, atmospheric pressure pushes water into the cylinder until the air pressure inside and outside the cylinder are balanced again.

Using this system, air pressure alone can be used to raise water 10 meters. By using a number of such pumps, water can be pumped from deep mines.

This important practical solution to a difficult problem also gave scientists some important clues about how the air behaved. The suction pump prompted both Galileo Galilei and Evangelista Torricelli to suggest that the air around us is under the pressure equivalent to a column of water 10 meters high.

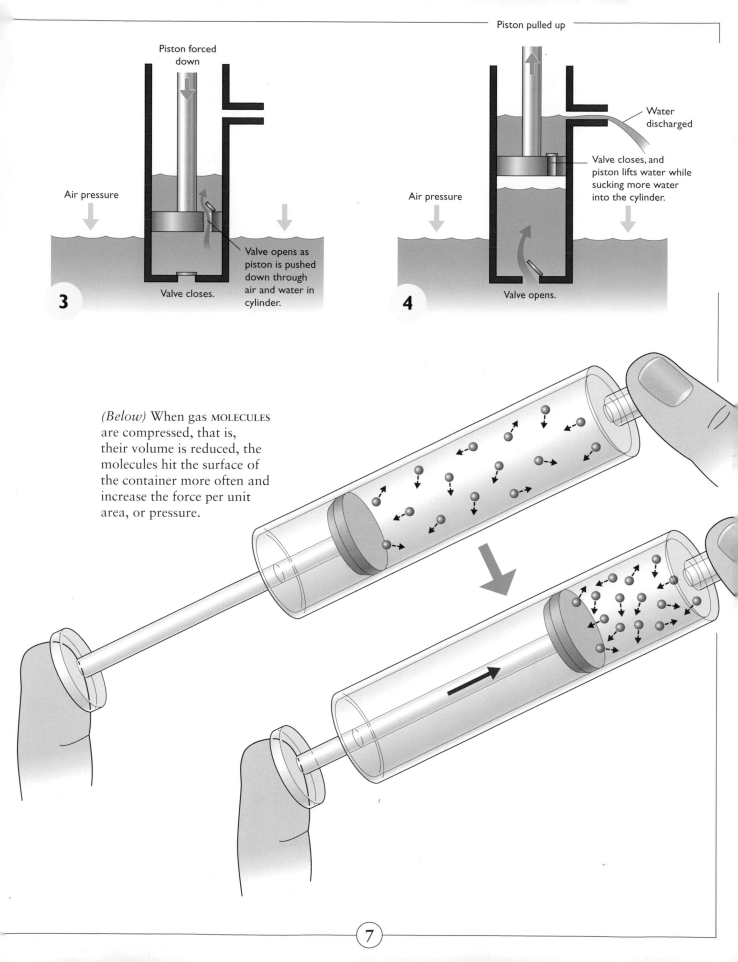

Piston forced down

Air pressure

3

Valve opens as piston is pushed down through air and water in cylinder.

Valve closes.

Piston pulled up

Water discharged

Valve closes, and piston lifts water while sucking more water into the cylinder.

Air pressure

4

Valve opens.

(Below) When gas MOLECULES are compressed, that is, their volume is reduced, the molecules hit the surface of the container more often and increase the force per unit area, or pressure.

Gas laws

In the 17th century Robert Boyle and Robert Hooke also developed the opposite of a suction, or VACUUM, pump—an air pump. An air pump like a bicycle pump compresses air and so increases its pressure. By experimenting with both air pumps and vacuum pumps, Boyle became convinced that gases were made of tiny independent particles of matter, which we now call ATOMS, and which he called "corpuscles."

This was of vital importance because it implied that all other kinds of matter were also made of atoms.

Sir Isaac Newton then showed mathematically that the properties of gases could be explained by assuming that they were atoms and that they repelled each other with increasing force as they came closer together.

By examining the way that gases change in pressure, temperature, and volume, Boyle was able to discover a simple relationship between the volume and pressure of a gas: If the gas volume (**V**) was halved by squashing it, the gas pressure (**P**) was doubled.

This can be stated as:

P is proportional to 1/V

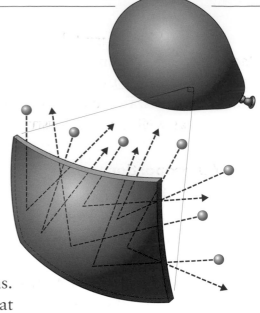

(Above) A balloon is kept inflated by the constant bombardment of its inner surface by air molecules under pressure.

(Below) Whenever you pump up a tire, you are proving Boyle's law. Because the volume of the tire is fixed, the more air that is pumped in, the higher the pressure becomes because more gas molecules are being confined in the same space. As a result, they collide with one another and with the tire walls more often, and that is what causes an increase in pressure.

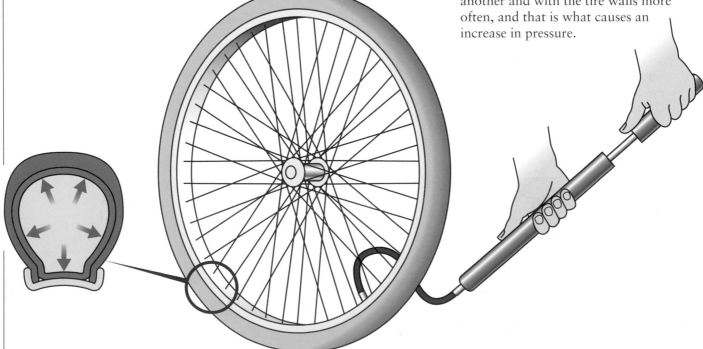

In the 18th century John Dalton, and later Jacques Charles, found more simple relationships between gases and their environment. They discovered that if a gas is warmed to temperature **T**, its volume **V** increases as well (and its DENSITY decreases).

Thus:

V is proportional to T

Today, this relationship is called Charles's law, although it was discovered first by Dalton.

Boyle's law and Charles's law are known as the gas laws, and they are remarkably simple and easy to use. When they are combined, we get the relationship:

PV is proportional to T or **PV = kT**

where **k** is a number that we can find by experiment.

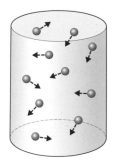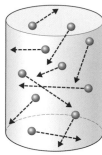

(Below) Heating a gas gives the molecules more energy, and they move faster—as a result, they hit the container with a greater speed and increase the pressure.

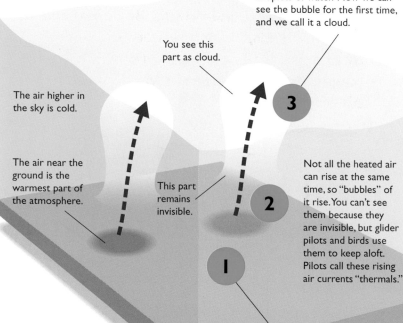

As the bubble rises, it cools and can hold less and less vapor.
  Finally, some vapor is converted into millions of tiny droplets of water. Now we can see the bubble for the first time, and we call it a cloud.

You see this part as cloud.

3

The air higher in the sky is cold.

The air near the ground is the warmest part of the atmosphere.

This part remains invisible.

2

1

Not all the heated air can rise at the same time, so "bubbles" of it rise. You can't see them because they are invisible, but glider pilots and birds use them to keep aloft. Pilots call these rising air currents "thermals."

(Right) We see evidence of the gas laws all around us. For example, on a sunny day air, on contact with the ground, is warmed. As a result, it increases its volume and becomes less dense. Because it is less dense, parts of this warm layer rise through the more dense colder air above it in the form of bubbles of air.

These rising bubbles of air are invisible to us except in certain circumstances. As the air rises, it cools, although it remains warmer than the air it is traveling through at every height. But eventually the water vapor contained in an air bubble begins to change to liquid droplets, and it is at this point that cloud forms.

On a warm day the Sun heats the ground. The warm ground shares its heat with the air above (this is just like the burner in the balloon).

This diagram shows how some types of clouds can be formed. It may help to imagine air bubbles as though they were many invisible hot-air balloons rising one after another.

The hydrogen gas that is given off is collected in a gas jar over water.

Zinc

(*Above*) The apparatus that you might use in a school laboratory today is shown for comparison to Hales' method (*below*).

(*Below*) Hales' method for collecting gases produced by chemical reactions led to the discovery of the things that make up air by providing a means of collecting gases for testing.

Through further studies of gases Dalton was able to deduce another important gas law: The total pressure of a mixture of gases equals the sum of the pressures of the gases in the mixture, each gas acting independently. This is called Dalton's law.

Collecting gases

Stephen Hales was the first person to collect a gas made of just one kind of atom (as opposed to the mixture of gases we call air). He filled a glass bottle with water and turned it over while the neck remained underwater. When the bottle was raised bottom upward out of the water, the inside remained full of water as long as the neck was held below the water level in the tank. This led him to develop an apparatus for collecting gases from chemical reactions. Gases emitted from substances in chemical reactions were collected in the bottle through a bent tube running from the glass vessel where the gases were produced.

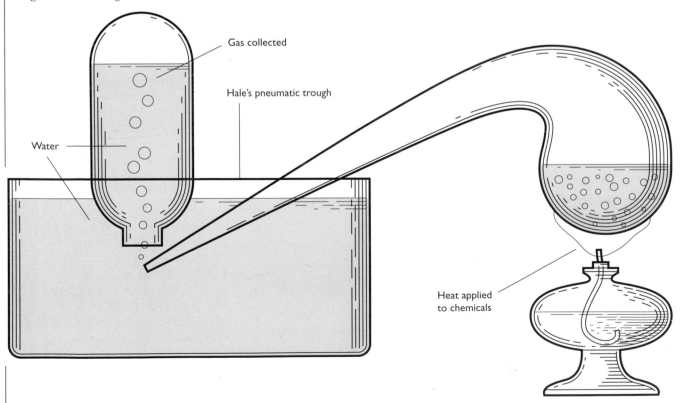

Gas collected

Hale's pneumatic trough

Water

Heat applied to chemicals

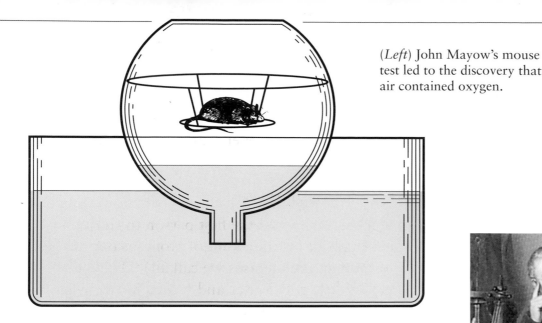

(*Left*) John Mayow's mouse test led to the discovery that air contained oxygen.

(*Above*) John Dalton (born 1766, died 1844) was a famous English scientist who studied, among other things, the nature of gases. He was, for the most part, self-educated, yet made major contributions to many fields of study, including the nature of the air.

In his research he made a practice of checking all of the facts for himself rather than relying on the accuracy of others just because they had published their results. He knew what is still true today, and that is that people can make mistakes and get things wrong.

He said: "Having been in my progress so often misled by taking for granted the results of others, I have determined to write as little as possible but what I can attest by my own experience."

Air, flames, and life

All of the early scientists studied air because it is connected to life and fire. In the 17th century, through experiments with dogs, Robert Hooke proved that the movements of breathing are not needed for life, and breathing is simply a kind of bellows whose purpose is to get air to the blood.

Boyle put candles and animals in vessels that could be connected to a vacuum pump. He discovered that if air was removed by the pump, the flames went out and the animal suffocated. As a result, he concluded that burning and living had something in common.

Also in the 17th century, John Mayow put a mouse in a jar of air inverted over a water tank. He noticed that the level of water gradually rose until the mouse died. That happened when water had occupied about a fourteenth part of the jar. From this he concluded that air contained something necessary for life. In doing this and in identifying what is now called oxygen as part of the air, he discovered what Joseph Priestley discovered a century later and is usually given credit for.

In the 18th century Priestley made many important contributions to the study of gases. He saw that the "foul air" that caused the mouse to die (and which we now understand is carbon dioxide) made a sprig of mint grow much faster than normal.

(*Below*) When red mercuric oxide (HgO) is heated, the powder first turns black and then decomposes into mercury and oxygen gas. In this test-tube experiment the mercury condenses on the cooler part of the tube, and the oxygen can be collected under water in a vessel similar to that developed by Hales (see page 10).

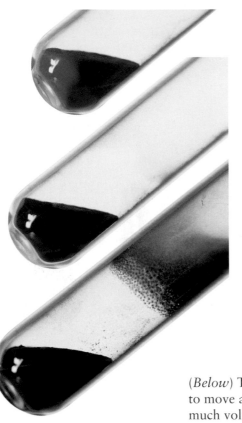

Also, when a mouse was put in the air that had previously been unsuitable for breathing, but in which mint had been growing for some time, the mouse could now thrive. From this he concluded that the freshness of the Earth's atmosphere is preserved by the Earth's plants and that there is a relationship between animal breathing (respiration), plant respiration, and the air.

It was Priestley who roasted red mercuric oxide and from it released and collected oxygen. Priestley at once recognized the gas as the part of the air that supports life and burning, and which is now called oxygen.

Properties of gases

From these and other, historic developments we now have a clear understanding of the properties of gases.

Gases are unattached molecules

Unlike SOLIDS, which have a fixed shape, and LIQUIDS, which always settle to fill the bottom of a container, gases have no particular shape or size but will adapt to fill any container they are put in.

Unless they are under pressure, gases occupy a hugely greater space than if the same number of MOLECULES were in liquid form. As a result, they are also

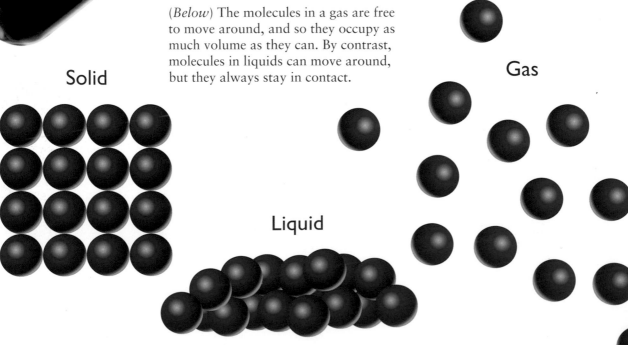

(*Below*) The molecules in a gas are free to move around, and so they occupy as much volume as they can. By contrast, molecules in liquids can move around, but they always stay in contact.

Solid

Gas

Liquid

far less able to resist the movement of an object (they are less VISCOUS) than liquids. For example, it is about a hundred times easier to force your way through air than through water.

Gases consist of a vast number of molecules moving randomly at very high speeds (about 500 m/s). As a result, molecules in a gas are constantly colliding. We do not notice this because there are so many molecules, and they are all so tiny. But we can sometimes witness it. For example, because the molecules are always moving very fast, they are able to fill any space very quickly.

Gases would spread out indefinitely if they were not held in a container. As they strike the walls of the container, they produce a force that we know as PRESSURE. The container does not have to be a solid.

(Below) In this demonstration a brown gas is placed in one flask and isolated from another flask by a clip in the connecting tube. The other flask is then emptied of gas using a vacuum pump. The clip is then removed with the result that the brown gas flashes into the evacuated flask almost instantly.

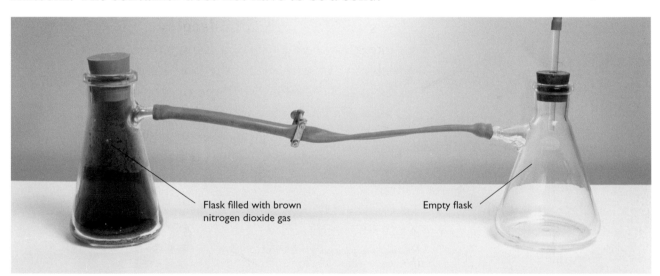

Flask filled with brown nitrogen dioxide gas

Empty flask

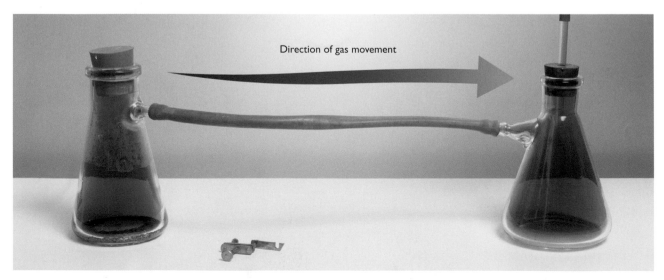

Direction of gas movement

Water holds air in bubbles; soap bubbles hold air in a film of soap. The container doesn't even have to be something physical: GRAVITY holds the gases of the air close to the Earth's surface to make the ATMOSPHERE (and so drives the suction pump as described on page 5).

Gases are elastic

If you squash a balloon by sitting on it, the air inside is compressed. If you then get up, the balloon regains its original size. It is sort of the same as stretching a rubber band and then watching it spring back into shape when you let go. This property of rebounding to the original shape is called ELASTICITY. Gases are elastic over their entire range. When they are squashed too much, they change into a liquid. Liquefying gases is a widespread industrial activity for separating the gases in the air (see page 36).

Gases produce a pressure

The pressure of a gas depends on the number of molecules colliding with the container it is in. If the gas is squashed, the number of molecules colliding with each square centimeter gets greater, and so the pressure goes up.

The presence of gas pressure (first seen in the suction pump) can be shown in many ways, such as by using a radiometer. It is a four-vaned "gas mill" that is enclosed in a glass container. One side of each vane is painted black; the other side is silvered. Most of the air is removed. When a strong light is shone onto the mill, the vanes begin to turn. That happens because the silvered side reflects away most of the energy, while the blackened side absorbs it and warms up. The air

(Below) A squashed balloon expands when the pressure is released.

molecules near the blackened vane warm up by CONDUCTION and gain more energy than the gas molecules near the silvered side. As a result, the collisions happen with more force on the blackened side, and that makes the vanes turn—but only if there are few enough molecules so that they collide with the vane more often than with each other. If all of the air is removed, the vanes stop turning because there is no gas to collide with the vanes and make them turn. If air is allowed in, the molecules of gas collide with one another so much that there are not enough to collide with the vanes and push them round.

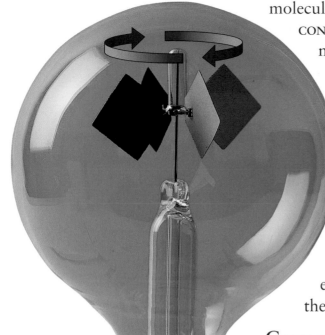

(Above) A radiometer is set spinning by gas pressure.

Gases can behave surprisingly

Gases behave sometimes in what appears to be the opposite of common sense. We might think, for example, the hotter a gas gets, the less thick it might become, and so the easier it would be to travel through it. After all, most liquids behave this way. But for gases the opposite is true: The hotter the gas, the more difficult it becomes to travel through it (with increasing temperature, the gas becomes more viscous).

Also, it is no easier to move through a DILUTE gas than it is through a concentrated gas. It makes no difference at all.

Third, if you mix two gases, for example, a dense one and a less dense one, instead of the stickiness of the mixture being somewhere between the two, the stickiness is actually greater than in either of the gases separately.

Another surprise is that if you take away some gas, the rest of the gas conducts heat in just the same way as when more gas is present. That is, changing the amount of gas does not affect the way gases conduct heat. Later on, we will see that this is important in thinking about insulation.

A gas also conducts heat better when it is hot than when it is cold.

From gas to liquid

Gases only survive if their molecules have enough energy to stay apart. If a gas is cooled, it loses energy; and at a particular temperature the gas suddenly turns into a liquid. This is called CONDENSATION.

We see condensation all around us, for example, when WATER VAPOR from the air condenses onto a glass of cold water. When this change takes place, the remaining energy in the gas is given out, even though the temperature of the gas remains the same until it has all turned to liquid. This energy is called LATENT HEAT.

On the other hand, if a liquid is warmed, it suddenly begins to boil and turn into a gas. Because a gas has more energy than a liquid, the liquid continues to boil at the same temperature until all of the liquid has turned into a gas. The extra latent heat energy needed for this change is taken from the source of heating.

Mixtures of gases

Gases rarely occur on their own but much more commonly stirred together, or as MIXTURES.

The properties of mixtures of gases contain some surprises, just as did individual gases.

(Above) Condensation on a glass. The diagram is not to scale.

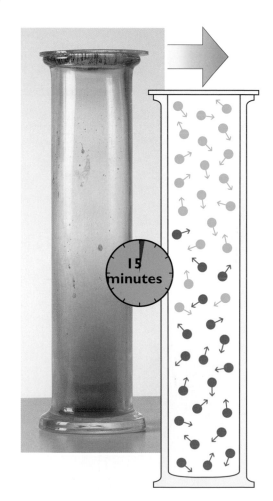

15 minutes

For example, we saw that gas molecules travel very fast. But we know from our experience that a smell, for example, only "wafts" across a room. That is because, although the gas molecules are moving very fast, their paths are continually blocked by other molecules, and they have to undergo many collisions with these other molecules in order to make any progress. In fact, a gas molecule may collide with other molecules over two trillion times and travel over 5,000 km just to make one meter of progress across a room! As a result, molecules actually move forward at an apparently much more leisurely speed. The process is called DIFFUSION, and it causes one gas to diffuse through another at a speed of just centimeters a second.

Another surprising thing is that the speed at which one gas moves through another is almost independent of the gases making up the mixture. So a smell would move at the same speed no matter what other gas it was going through.

(Below) Diffusion of one gas through another is a slow process, as shown by the brown and colorless gases in this gas jar.

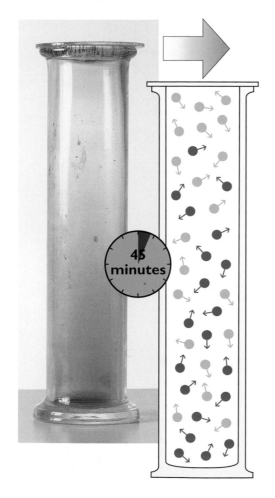

45 minutes

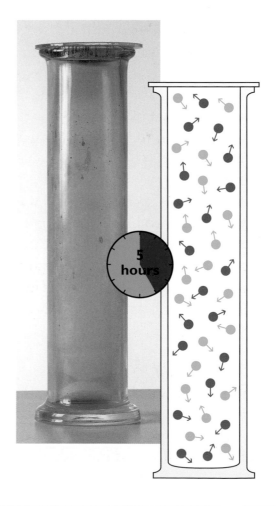

5 hours

2: Air

The air is a mixture of gases, which means that the air is made up of molecules belonging to a number of gases that do not react with one another. The exceptions to this are the gases that pour into the air from pollution, and we will look at them later.

The main unvarying gases are these (as percentages by volume):

Nitrogen (N_2)	78.084
Oxygen (O_2)	20.946
Argon (Ar)	0.934
Neon (Ne)	0.0018
Helium (He)	0.000524
Methane (CH_4)	0.0002
Krypton (Kr)	0.000114
Hydrogen (H_2)	0.00005
Nitrous oxide (N_2O)	0.00005
Xenon (Xe)	0.0000087

The air around us makes up the ATMOSPHERE. The atmosphere is heated by contact with the ground below. The air is not primarily heated directly by the Sun. The atmosphere also loses heat to space so that over time, the average temperature of the atmosphere stays the same.

The atmosphere is heated more strongly near the equator than at the poles. This imbalance makes air move in a process called CONVECTION, in which hot air rises and moves poleward, balanced by cold air sinking and moving to the equator.

Because the Earth is spinning, the movement of air between the pole and equator is changed into a pattern of complicated spirals, of which hurricanes are the most dramatic examples.

The churning movement of the air in the atmosphere helps mix all of the air in the lower

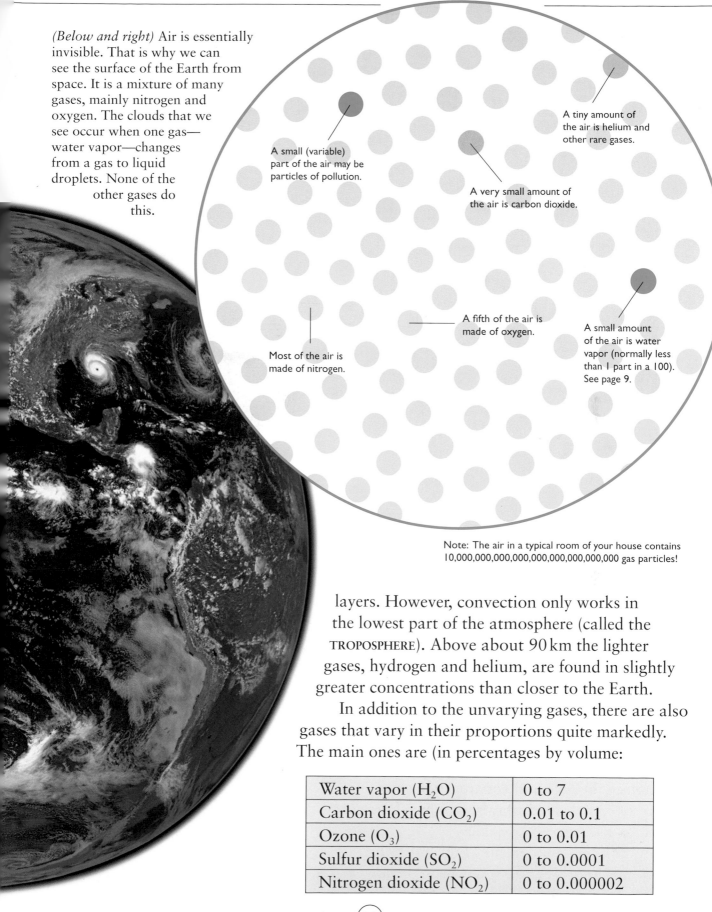

(Below and right) Air is essentially invisible. That is why we can see the surface of the Earth from space. It is a mixture of many gases, mainly nitrogen and oxygen. The clouds that we see occur when one gas—water vapor—changes from a gas to liquid droplets. None of the other gases do this.

A small (variable) part of the air may be particles of pollution.

A tiny amount of the air is helium and other rare gases.

A very small amount of the air is carbon dioxide.

A fifth of the air is made of oxygen.

A small amount of the air is water vapor (normally less than 1 part in a 100). See page 9.

Most of the air is made of nitrogen.

Note: The air in a typical room of your house contains 10,000,000,000,000,000,000,000,000,000 gas particles!

layers. However, convection only works in the lowest part of the atmosphere (called the TROPOSPHERE). Above about 90 km the lighter gases, hydrogen and helium, are found in slightly greater concentrations than closer to the Earth.

In addition to the unvarying gases, there are also gases that vary in their proportions quite markedly. The main ones are (in percentages by volume:

Water vapor (H_2O)	0 to 7
Carbon dioxide (CO_2)	0.01 to 0.1
Ozone (O_3)	0 to 0.01
Sulfur dioxide (SO_2)	0 to 0.0001
Nitrogen dioxide (NO_2)	0 to 0.000002

(*Below*) The atmosphere is the envelope around the Earth that contains a significant amount of gas. Only the lowest layer, the troposphere, has enough oxygen to support life.

Exosphere (above 600 km from the Earth's surface). Air molecules are very rare at these levels, and helium is the most common gas.

Thermosphere (about 500 km thick). Extremely thin air. Readily absorbs ultraviolet radiation. Within this layer lies the ionosphere, the place that bounces back medium and short radio waves, allowing them to travel large distances around the world.

Mesosphere (about 50 km thick). Transparent to the Sun's rays. Temperature decreases with height.

Stratosphere (about 30 km thick). Contains important ozone gas. Temperature increases with height.

Troposphere (10 to 20 km thick—thickest over the equator, thinnest at the poles). The layer that contains the clouds and most of the oxygen. It is mainly transparent to the Sun's rays. The temperature decreases with height.

None of these gases occurs in large amounts, but each has a disproportionate influence on life on Earth.

Water vapor not only absorbs heat radiated from the Earth's surface and helps raise the air temperature (the GREENHOUSE EFFECT—see page 49), but it also produces rain, essential for plant growth on land.

Carbon dioxide is also able to absorb heat and contribute to the greenhouse effect. It is also the source of carbon for plant growth and so plays a vital role in PHOTOSYNTHESIS.

Ozone in the upper atmosphere traps ultraviolet radiation, protecting living things from potentially harmful rays.

Sulfur dioxide and nitrogen dioxide are the principal gases produced by the combustion of fuels. We know them as the gases that can be responsible for ACID RAIN (see page 46). However, both gases are also produced naturally, for example, when oxygen and nitrogen in the air react under the incredibly high temperatures that occur during a flash of lightning.

For most practical purposes each of these gases is INERT and allows air to be used as though it were a single substance, as we shall see below. Only water vapor changes the properties of the air significantly, and that only when the amount of water vapor is so great that it is close to its saturation level (known as "wet" air). For this reason we need to distinguish between "dry air" and "wet air." The properties below refer to dry air unless stated to the contrary.

An electrical insulating material

Dry air—air—is an excellent electrical insulator. However, water (containing impurities) is a good conductor of electricity, so the higher the water vapor content of the air, the less insulating the air is. Lightning flashes actually take place between the ground and layers of cloud under conditions of high humidity (wet air).

(Right) A printed circuit board uses exposed metal conductors. It relies on the insulating properties of the air to save on the trouble and expense of having to sheath all connections in, for example, plastic.

(Above) Air is widely used as an insulator. The ceramic insulators shown here are just used to separate the cables from the metal of the pylon. The air provides the insulation between the cables and the ground.

Air is one of the most useful insulators. It is used, for example, to insulate cables carrying high-voltage electricity from the ground. Because of the naturally great insulation properties of air, the high-voltage cables can be left unsheathed and simply slung through the air between pylons. In this way air provides free insulation and cuts down the cost of other forms of insulation.

In a similar way the insulating properties of air are vital in allowing electrical and electronic components to be placed close to one another without the need for extra insulation. For example, printed circuit boards carry exposed metal wires and rely entirely on the natural insulation of air to prevent short circuits.

A heat insulator

Heat is transferred by the three processes already referred to: conduction, convection, and RADIATION. Air is an excellent heat insulator; but if it moves, it will transfer heat quite rapidly. So, the key to using air as an insulator is to prevent it from moving. That is why most clothes or building materials are designed to trap air and keep it from moving around.

(Left and below) Clothes, like home insulation, trap air and use its great insulating properties.

Moisture goes through, but air is trapped by the fibers.

Air is used, for example, in most buildings and in all of our clothes. We may look at our clothes and see layers of fibers that we think keep us warm or see in a building two layers of glass that we call double glazing. But in both cases the insulation material is actually air. The wool, bricks, fiberglass, or other materials just provide the scaffolding to trap the air and keep it from moving.

(Right) Multiple layers of fiber are good for insulation in a ski glove, but only because they trap more air than a single layer. In a similar way wearing several lightweight sweaters is a more effective way of keeping warm than wearing a single heavyweight sweater.

Heated air goes through pillared chambers in the hypocaust, providing underfloor heating.

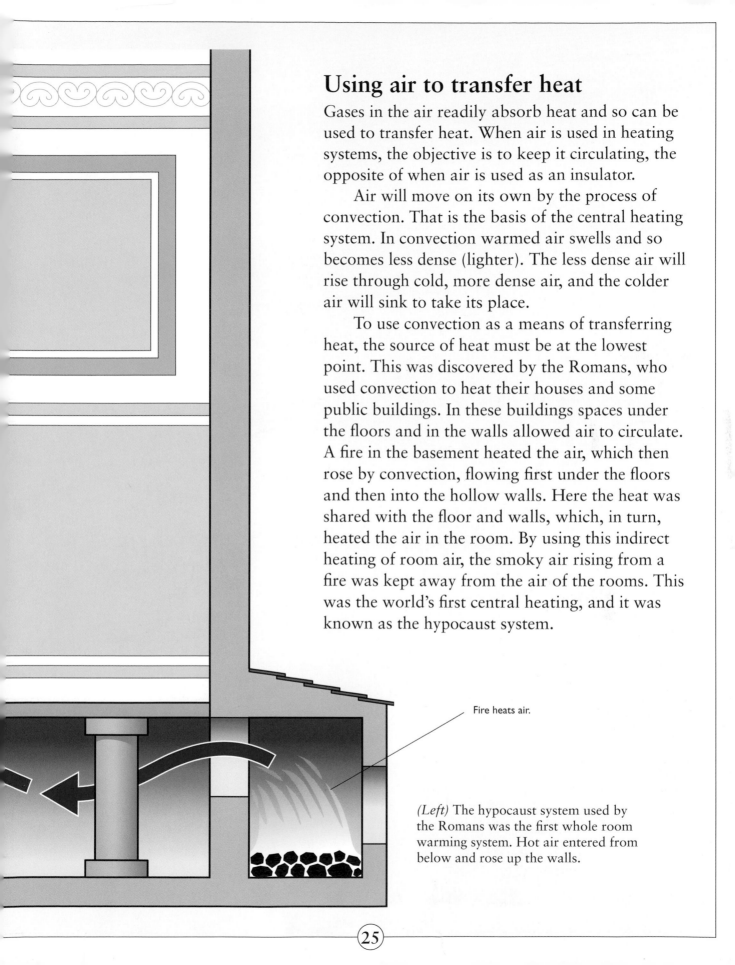

Using air to transfer heat

Gases in the air readily absorb heat and so can be used to transfer heat. When air is used in heating systems, the objective is to keep it circulating, the opposite of when air is used as an insulator.

Air will move on its own by the process of convection. That is the basis of the central heating system. In convection warmed air swells and so becomes less dense (lighter). The less dense air will rise through cold, more dense air, and the colder air will sink to take its place.

To use convection as a means of transferring heat, the source of heat must be at the lowest point. This was discovered by the Romans, who used convection to heat their houses and some public buildings. In these buildings spaces under the floors and in the walls allowed air to circulate. A fire in the basement heated the air, which then rose by convection, flowing first under the floors and then into the hollow walls. Here the heat was shared with the floor and walls, which, in turn, heated the air in the room. By using this indirect heating of room air, the smoky air rising from a fire was kept away from the air of the rooms. This was the world's first central heating, and it was known as the hypocaust system.

Fire heats air.

(Left) The hypocaust system used by the Romans was the first whole room warming system. Hot air entered from below and rose up the walls.

Air can also be blown over a cold or hot element to cool or heat the air by conduction. This is air conditioning. Air conditioning in modern housing is similar to the hypocaust system insofar as air is heated at a central location (as opposed to radiators in each room). But the difference is that it is then forced by fans through tubes, or ducts, so that it rises along the walls of each room. A separate set of ducts allows cold air to return for heating. Forced air central heating has the advantage for offices, for example, of being able to be cleaned and its relative humidity controlled as the warm or cold air circulates.

(*Below*) An air-conditioning system involves three parts: a source of temperature-controlled air, the rooms that the air should flow through, and an extractor unit to remove the air. This diagram (not to scale) shows a direct through-flow system.

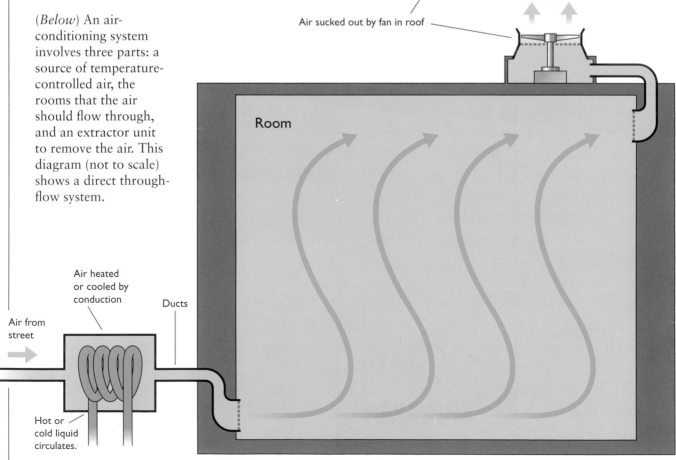

Air sucked out by fan in roof

Air

Room

Air heated or cooled by conduction

Ducts

Air from street

Hot or cold liquid circulates.

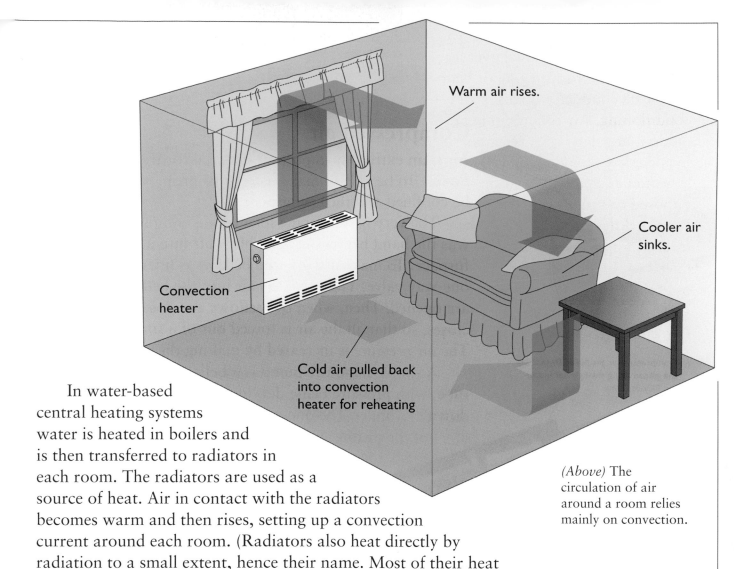

Warm air rises.

Cooler air sinks.

Convection heater

Cold air pulled back into convection heater for reheating

(Above) The circulation of air around a room relies mainly on convection.

In water-based central heating systems water is heated in boilers and is then transferred to radiators in each room. The radiators are used as a source of heat. Air in contact with the radiators becomes warm and then rises, setting up a convection current around each room. (Radiators also heat directly by radiation to a small extent, hence their name. Most of their heat is, however, transferred by convection.)

Electric "convection" heaters are usually designed as a vertical chimney with the heating element at the bottom. In this system there is no heat exchange by radiation at all. In other respects a convection heater acts in the same way as a radiator.

Radiators and convection heaters are usually set either below windows or along external walls. That is because they are naturally cold surfaces, and air in contact with them will become colder, denser and therefore begin to sink, causing drafts.

Hot-air blowers are used in many stores and industrial buildings. In this case the air is blown over the fins of a heater. This transfers heat by conduction and then blows it into the room. As a result, the heater does not need to be set at the bottom of a wall but is usually put above head height and the air blown downward.

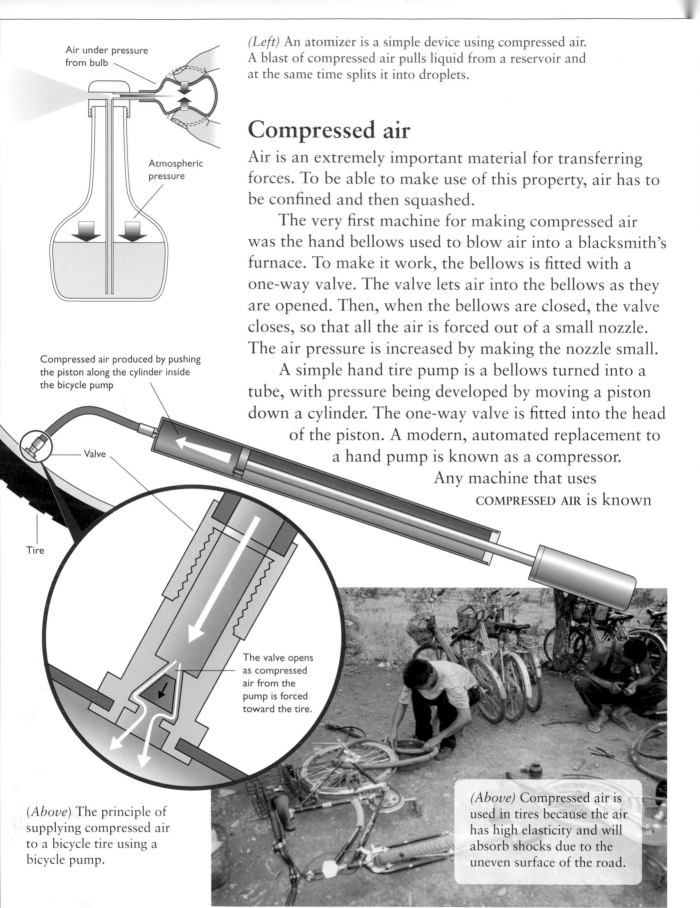

(*Left*) An atomizer is a simple device using compressed air. A blast of compressed air pulls liquid from a reservoir and at the same time splits it into droplets.

Air under pressure from bulb

Atmospheric pressure

Compressed air

Air is an extremely important material for transferring forces. To be able to make use of this property, air has to be confined and then squashed.

The very first machine for making compressed air was the hand bellows used to blow air into a blacksmith's furnace. To make it work, the bellows is fitted with a one-way valve. The valve lets air into the bellows as they are opened. Then, when the bellows are closed, the valve closes, so that all the air is forced out of a small nozzle. The air pressure is increased by making the nozzle small.

A simple hand tire pump is a bellows turned into a tube, with pressure being developed by moving a piston down a cylinder. The one-way valve is fitted into the head of the piston. A modern, automated replacement to a hand pump is known as a compressor.

Any machine that uses COMPRESSED AIR is known

Compressed air produced by pushing the piston along the cylinder inside the bicycle pump

Valve

Tire

The valve opens as compressed air from the pump is forced toward the tire.

(*Above*) The principle of supplying compressed air to a bicycle tire using a bicycle pump.

(*Above*) Compressed air is used in tires because the air has high elasticity and will absorb shocks due to the uneven surface of the road.

as a PNEUMATIC DEVICE. You will find pneumatic devices in many places. A tire, for example, is inflated with compressed air to support and cushion the weight of a vehicle. The brakes on trucks, trains, and buses operate with compressed air. A jet engine in an aircraft also has air compressors. A paint sprayer relies on a jet of compressed air to suck paint from a reservoir and spray it evenly onto surfaces. A pneumatic drill takes compressed air to make a chisel jump up and down and so break through concrete or

(Below) How a pneumatic drill works.

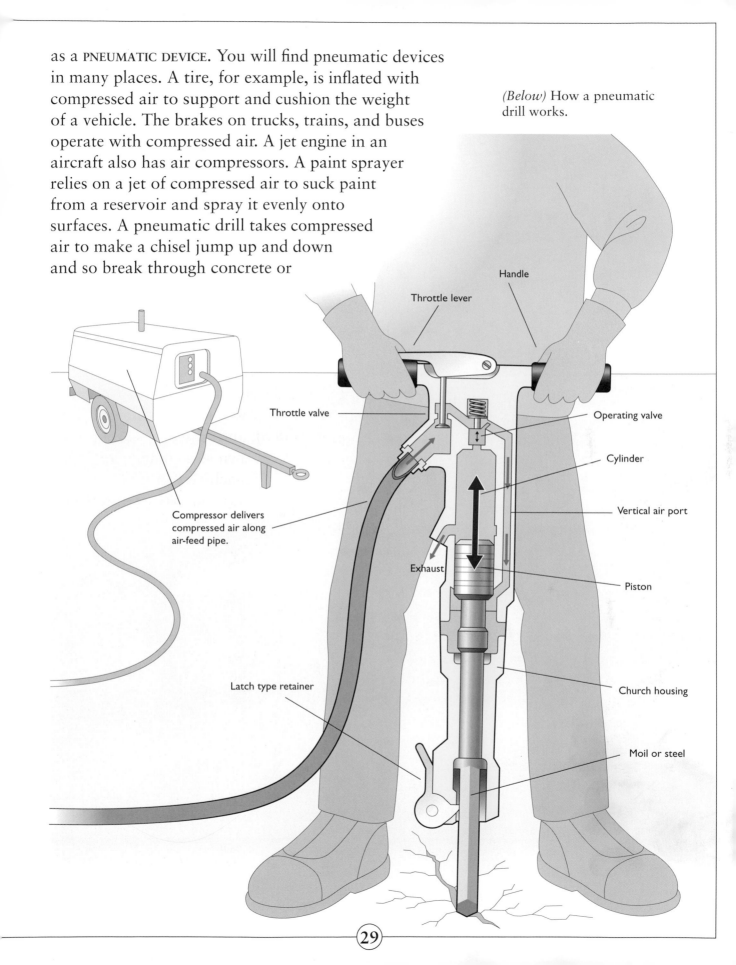

Handle

Throttle lever

Throttle valve

Operating valve

Cylinder

Vertical air port

Compressor delivers compressed air along air-feed pipe.

Exhaust

Piston

Latch type retainer

Church housing

Moil or steel

(Left) Large compressed air drills are used in mining. Rock can be chipped away or holes bored to take explosives.

smash rocks. A garage has a pneumatic wrench for tightening or loosening nuts. A riveter fastens pieces of sheet metal together with a pneumatic tool, and a person cleaning a building uses a pneumatic tool to sand or water blast the dirty surface.

The reason that pneumatic, or compressed air, power is so common is that the resource needed—air—is all around. It is a safe material and cheap to run. Pneumatic devices work in places where electric devices might be a danger. For example, in mining, an electric motor might produce a spark that could ignite any explosive gases in the mine. A pneumatic drill produces no sparks and so is much safer. Similarly, an electric motor cannot be run when it is wet because of the danger of a short circuit and the chance of the operator being electrocuted.

Another advantage of compressed air is that the compressor can be small and still run powerful devices. Usually, compressed air is built up in a large tank using a small compressor. When the air is needed, for example, to drive a pneumatic drill, all of the air in the tank is available. Then, when the drill is stopped, the small compressor can continue

(Below) Robotically controlled or less sophisticated hand-operated compressed air paint applicators such as these are used on production lines.

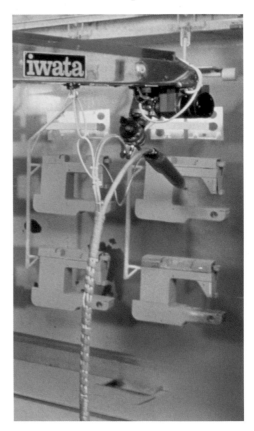

to replenish the tank ready for the next period of demand.

Compressed air is even more flexible because it can be treated much like water. That is, you do not need to have just one device connected to a tank of compressed air. Hundreds of devices can be connected to the same reservoir of air using flexible hoses or rigid tubes. Because air will be at the same pressure everywhere in the hose or pipe system, any or all of the devices can work at full power at the same time. All that is needed is a coupling device, such as a valve and suitable socket.

Thus, although the compressor may be run by an electric motor, the motor does not have to be anywhere near the operating device. Motors can, for example, be located above ground and compressed air tools used below ground in a mine.

A compressed air system is very trouble free because there are few moving parts, while the pressure going to the device can be controlled with great precision.

Machines can be made to work by allowing compressed air to push on vanes that are attached to a spindle. That rotates (turns) the spindle. Speed of rotation is controlled by adjusting the flow of air. This is the kind of device that might operate a factory drill.

In a train brake or a pneumatic drill the air pushes on a piston, forcing it along a cylinder. When the air is switched off, a spring returns the piston to its starting position.

Interestingly, many kinds of material can be moved within a system of pipes in which compressed air is moving. For example, ashes can be transported from a power plant furnace to a disposal site.

Other types of use are described in the following sections.

Grinding wheel

Air motor

Switch

(Above) Pneumatic grinders use compressed air to drive the motor.

(Above) Many dentists' drills run on compressed air.

Using air in transportation

Air can be used for transportation in a number ways: Moving air can directly support a vehicle, as in hovercraft, or the air can support a vehicle by moving quickly through it, as in aircraft.

Hovercrafts

Hovercrafts are vehicles that use powerful fans to force air out under their bottoms. The reaction of the air blowing on the ground is to lift the craft a small distance from the ground.

The concept of the hovercraft came partly from much earlier developments with aircraft. When an aircraft flies close to the ground, the wings get much more lift than when the craft is high in the air. The wind and the ground create a funnel effect, making the air pressure greater as the plane flies close to the ground. Early flying boats made use of this effect by skimming close to the sea surface. The result was better fuel economy.

Weight of hovercraft

(Above) The hovercraft principle can be demonstrated with a simple paper and board model.

(Right) The hovercraft principle. Giant fans force air under the skirt. That increases the pressure under the hovercraft until it is enough to lift the hovercraft off the ground.

Christopher Cockerell in England developed the Hovercraft, an air-cushion vehicle, in the 1950s. In his design air is pumped under the craft through a narrow slot running around the outside edge of the hull. In a classic kitchen table experiment Cockerell used a blower that fed air into an upturned coffee can, which had a hole in the base. The can was suspended over the weighing pan of a pair of kitchen scales. When the blower was turned on, air blown into the tin forced the pan down against the mass of a number of weights. Then he attached a second tin inside the first to leave a small slot all the way around the outside. When the blower was turned on, the force generated supported over three times more mass than when a single can was used.

Cockerell first developed this idea to allow boats to go faster by getting some of the hull out of the water. But then he realized that the same craft could be used on land, making them AMPHIBIOUS vehicles. To make it easier to move over irregular ground, the bottom of the sides of the hull was fitted with a rubber skirt. It allowed the air to stay trapped under the craft even when the land was uneven.

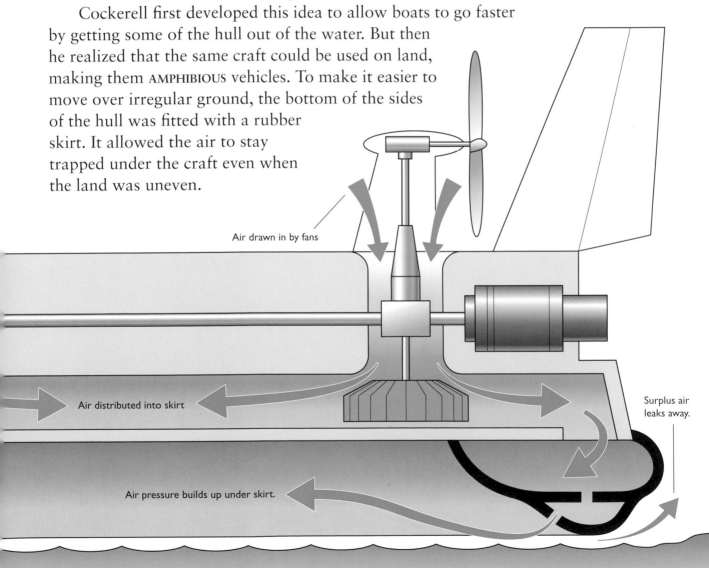

Air drawn in by fans

Air distributed into skirt

Surplus air leaks away.

Air pressure builds up under skirt.

The same principle was used later to build rigid sidewall craft. They are designed for use in the water only, with the skirt under water. The advantage is that these craft are more stable than a hovercraft and can use propellers in the water rather than the fans needed to blow air for movement in a hovercraft.

Air cushions

Once the ideas of hovercraft were put into practice, others began to see the potential for reducing friction by using air support. Prominent among them was the air-cushion train.

Air cushions have also proved valuable to support and move heavy loads in places where wheeled or tracked vehicles could not go. One such is a heavy load carrier, designed to spread the weight of a heavy load when going over a weak bridge. Without such a vehicle the cost of strengthening the bridge would be enormous. In this case a skirt and blower system are attached to an ordinary truck. Air-cushion vehicles are also widely used by oil exploration and other crews in the Arctic where ordinary vehicles would cause great environmental damage. Air-cushion vehicles are also cheaper to build and run than helicopters.

In factories loads are sometimes carried on air-cushion pallets.

Aircraft lift

When an aircraft travels quickly through the air, the wings give it lift. It is produced by the wing shape. The wing splits the airflow and causes

(Below) When an aircraft wing moves through air, it makes the air diverge so that there is a lack of air above the wing. This is shown by the smoke trails in this wind tunnel.

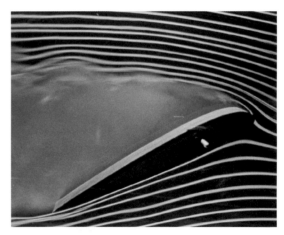

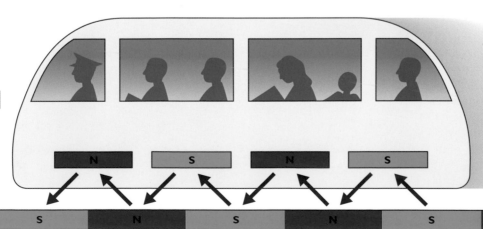

(Left) Magnets can be used to levitate and propel special trains.

more air to go under the wing than above it. This produces a lack of air (and so a partial vacuum) above the wing and a surplus of air (and so the equivalent of compressed air) below it. The imbalance produces an uplift force on the wing. The amount of uplift force is controlled in part by the speed of the aircraft and in part by the shape of the wing. Flaps on the wing are used to make small corrections to the lifting force.

Air brake

Air can be used for braking in two different ways: Heavy trucks, buses, and trains have air brakes that force brake pads against the wheels using compressed air. This system was invented by George Westinghouse in about 1860 for stopping trains. It is a much more powerful braking system than is used on cars.

Air brakes are also used by aircraft. In this case the objective is to increase the amount of air resistance that an aircraft can produce as it comes in to land. An air brake in this context is a flap that is raised above and lowered below the wing.

(Below) Airbrakes use air pressure to force a brake pad against a wheel.

Wheel

Air supply

Piston

Cylinder

Brake pad

(Above) Aircraft wing brakes in action on landing. The flaps disrupt the air flow, reduce lift, and at the same time produce more air resistance, so slowing down the aircraft.

Air gun

The first air guns used compressed air. When the trigger was pulled, the air was released, and that fired the shot. Later, this system was replaced by one in which the trigger actuated a spring that pushed a piston into a cylinder, and that then fired the shot.

3: Gases from the air

The air is a mixture of gases, and so the gases can be extracted and used as materials in their own right. The easiest way to do this is to cool down air so that each of the gases liquefies. Since this happens at different temperatures, each gas can be liquefied separately. For example, nitrogen has a boiling point of −196°C and oxygen −183°C. At the same time, liquefying the gases dramatically reduces their volume and makes them easier to store and transport.

(Right) Certain plants such as peas and beans have root nodules containing bacteria that fix nitrogen into nitrogen compounds. Plants such as these are often used by farmers to add nitrogen compounds to soils that have had these nutrients removed by successive crops.

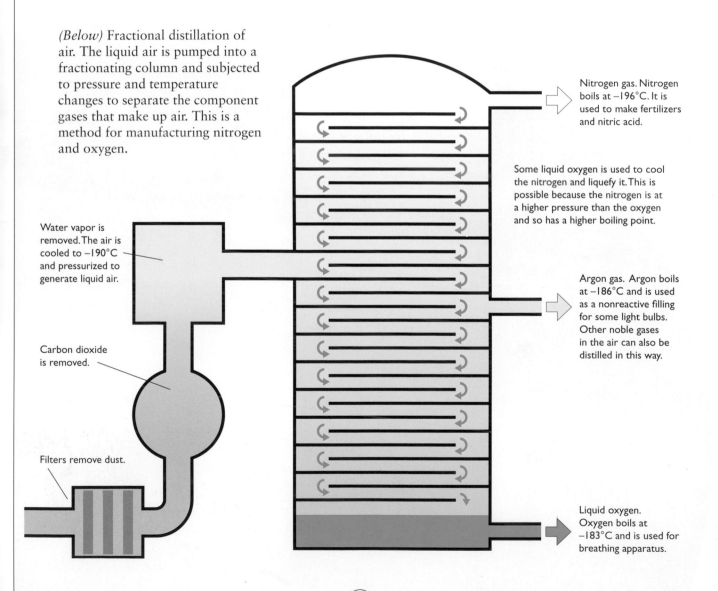

(Below) Fractional distillation of air. The liquid air is pumped into a fractionating column and subjected to pressure and temperature changes to separate the component gases that make up air. This is a method for manufacturing nitrogen and oxygen.

Water vapor is removed. The air is cooled to −190°C and pressurized to generate liquid air.

Carbon dioxide is removed.

Filters remove dust.

Nitrogen gas. Nitrogen boils at −196°C. It is used to make fertilizers and nitric acid.

Some liquid oxygen is used to cool the nitrogen and liquefy it. This is possible because the nitrogen is at a higher pressure than the oxygen and so has a higher boiling point.

Argon gas. Argon boils at −186°C and is used as a nonreactive filling for some light bulbs. Other noble gases in the air can also be distilled in this way.

Liquid oxygen. Oxygen boils at −183°C and is used for breathing apparatus.

Nitrogen

Seventy-eight percent of the atmosphere by volume is composed of nitrogen, that is, it is by far the most important part of the mixture we call air. Nitrogen is a colorless, odorless, and tasteless gas. It occurs in molecules made of pairs of atoms and is shown by the chemical symbol N_2.

Nitrogen is a very unreactive gas (and thus quite different from oxygen, see below). In terms of the atmosphere nitrogen is simply a "filler," making up most of the air pressure but having nothing much to do with absorbing heat, reacting with light, or changing in ways that some other atmospheric gases do. As a result, the French chemist Antoine Lavoisier, who first recognized the gas, named it azote (from the Greek "against life") because it is not able to support life. The name nitrogen comes from the fact that the gas is found in a substance once called niter (potassium nitrate). "Gen" means "forming."

Nitrogen in the air is indirectly important to life because nitrogen atoms make up part of all plant and animal tissues. Nitrogen gets to plants from the air in two ways. Bacteria are able to take nitrogen from the air and form it into a liquid compound that plants can absorb through their roots. Gases that are oxides of nitrogen are also produced during volcanic eruptions. They are soluble and so can be washed from the air into the soil.

(Below) Lightning causes oxygen to react with nitrogen. The oxides produced are then dissolved in rainfall.

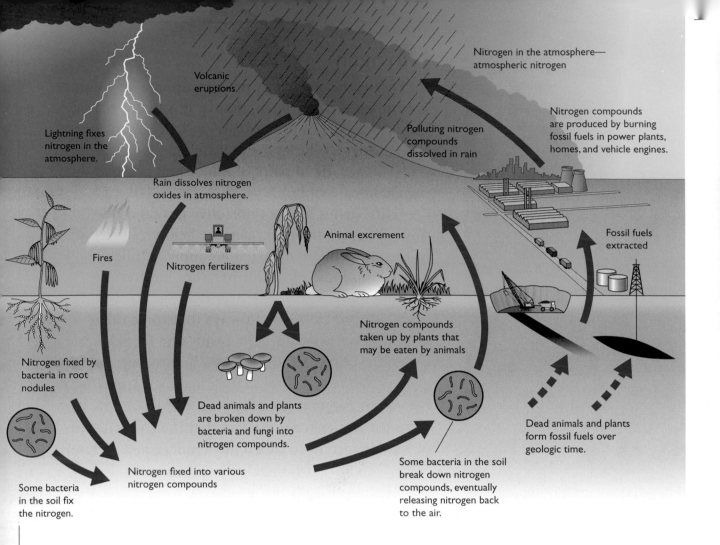

Nitrogen in the atmosphere— atmospheric nitrogen

Volcanic eruptions

Lightning fixes nitrogen in the atmosphere.

Polluting nitrogen compounds dissolved in rain

Nitrogen compounds are produced by burning fossil fuels in power plants, homes, and vehicle engines.

Rain dissolves nitrogen oxides in atmosphere.

Fossil fuels extracted

Fires

Animal excrement

Nitrogen fertilizers

Nitrogen fixed by bacteria in root nodules

Nitrogen compounds taken up by plants that may be eaten by animals

Dead animals and plants are broken down by bacteria and fungi into nitrogen compounds.

Dead animals and plants form fossil fuels over geologic time.

Some bacteria in the soil fix the nitrogen.

Nitrogen fixed into various nitrogen compounds

Some bacteria in the soil break down nitrogen compounds, eventually releasing nitrogen back to the air.

(*Above*) The nitrogen cycle.

(*Below*) Bacteria and fungi break down organic compounds containing nitrogen to release nitrogen to the air.

Nitrogen and air pollution

Although nitrogen does not readily combine with oxygen in the air, oxides of nitrogen produced by chemical reactions (for example, in car engines) can react strongly with oxygen in the air. The oxides of nitrogen produced are known collectively as Nox.

Air can become polluted by nitrogen oxides without it being obvious because many gases are colorless, odorless, and tasteless, especially in tiny concentrations. However, such concentrations, however tiny, can still have a major impact on our environment.

Some cities, such as Los Angeles, Mexico City, Tokyo, and Bangkok, which lie in areas of calm air and are often visited by sinking air conditions called ANTICYCLONES, are especially prone to this pollution

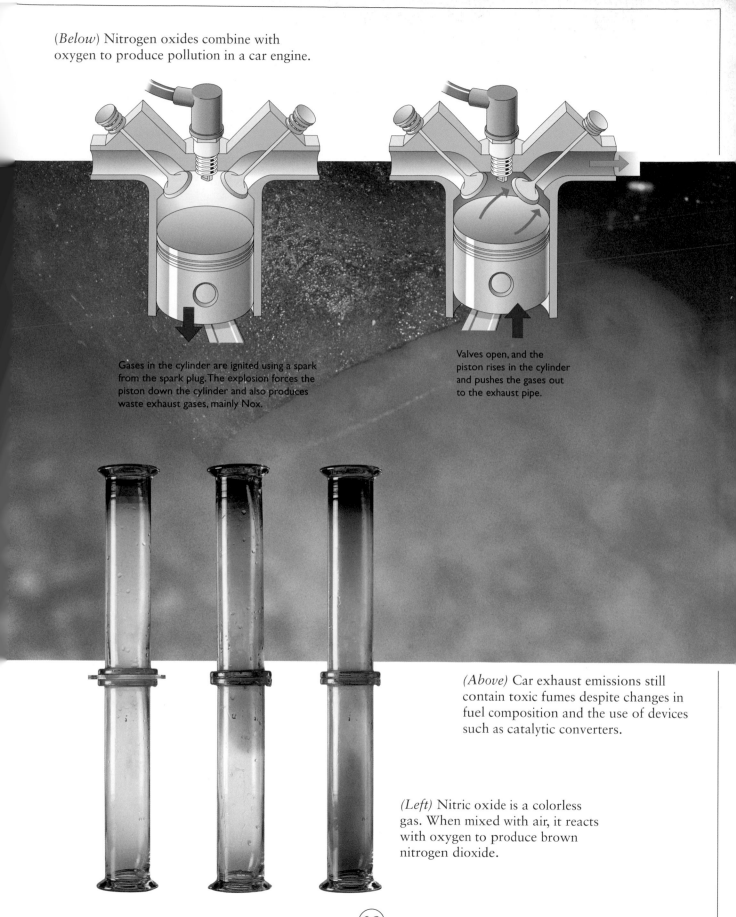

(*Below*) Nitrogen oxides combine with oxygen to produce pollution in a car engine.

Gases in the cylinder are ignited using a spark from the spark plug. The explosion forces the piston down the cylinder and also produces waste exhaust gases, mainly Nox.

Valves open, and the piston rises in the cylinder and pushes the gases out to the exhaust pipe.

(*Above*) Car exhaust emissions still contain toxic fumes despite changes in fuel composition and the use of devices such as catalytic converters.

(*Left*) Nitric oxide is a colorless gas. When mixed with air, it reacts with oxygen to produce brown nitrogen dioxide.

problem. Here, the sunshine causes the Nox in the air to react and produce new gases, including brown (poisonous) nitrogen dioxide. This produces what is known as PHOTOCHEMICAL SMOG.

Cleaning the air that leaves vehicle exhaust pipes can only be partly controlled. Catalytic converters are now attached to all cars in most developed countries. They turn many of the Nox gases that would normally become pollutants into those that are harmless.

(Above) Nitrogen can keep foods fresh by excluding air. It is widely used in snack packets.

(Below) Photochemical smog over Los Angeles.

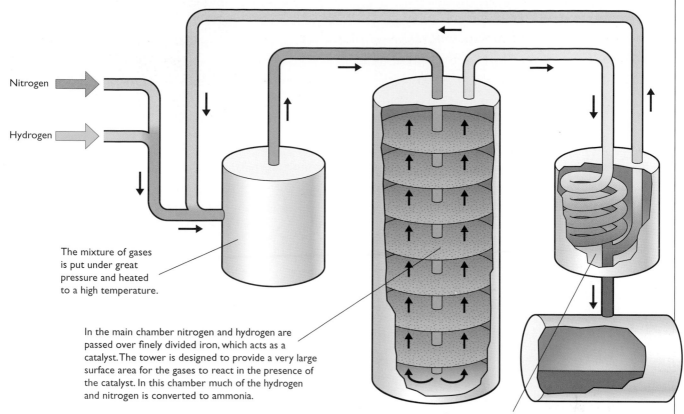

Nitrogen

Hydrogen

The mixture of gases is put under great pressure and heated to a high temperature.

In the main chamber nitrogen and hydrogen are passed over finely divided iron, which acts as a catalyst. The tower is designed to provide a very large surface area for the gases to react in the presence of the catalyst. In this chamber much of the hydrogen and nitrogen is converted to ammonia.

The gases are cooled, and ammonia liquefies and is drawn off from the base of the cooling chamber. The unreacted gases are recycled back to the catalytic chamber.

(*Above*) Nitrogen is used as a raw material for making ammonia in the Haber-Bosch process.

Uses of nitrogen

Nitrogen gas makes nitrates (which are fertilizers) and some plastics.

Strangely, nitrogen can be useful simply because it is inert and does not react with other substances. For instance, nitrogen is used in many factories that process foods. By keeping oxygen away from the foods, the foods stay fresher for longer. You will find nitrogen, for example, in many bags of chips (the nitrogen is what makes the bags stay puffed up).

Nitrogen also helps freeze-dry food because, unlike air, it contains no moisture. It is also a refrigerant when perishable goods are transported.

Another important use of nitrogen gas is in a reaction with hydrogen to produce ammonia. Ammonia is then made into a fertilizer and nitric acid.

(*Below*) An Ethiopian farmer adds a pellet of fertilizer (left hand) to each grain of corn to help the crop's growth.

Air bags

The so-called "air bag," which is used to help protect passengers in a vehicle accident, does not, in fact, use air but is inflated on impact by an explosion that produces nitrogen gas. A crash sensor sends an electrical signal to an igniter, which triggers an explosion of nitrogen compounds. This produces nitrogen gas to inflate the air bag in about 40 thousandths of a second.

However, it is not a rigid bag because if it were, it might cause as much damage as no bag. Instead, the bag has a pattern of holes in it that allow the gas to come out as the passenger is thrown forward or sideways during the accident. The bag deflates through these holes within one or two seconds. By forcing the air out through the holes, the bag absorbs much of the energy of the passenger's movement.

Because the gas used is nitrogen, it is inert and cannot add to any fire risk or suffocate the passenger. The air bags are normally hidden in the steering column or dashboard and also in side panels of the front seats. They protect the person from front and side impact.

Nitrogen and the bends

Although it performs no useful role as a gas in living things, nitrogen, like other gases, does become dissolved in the blood of animals. As the pressure increases, the amount of nitrogen that becomes dissolved increases quickly. If the pressure is then reduced, the nitrogen turns back into gas form. For divers returning from deep dives this gives a risk of bubbles forming in the blood, something called "the bends" (decompression sickness), which can be fatal.

(Below) How an air bag works with nitrogen gas.

A crash sensor is a steel ball that slides inside a smooth tube. The ball is held in place by a permanent magnet. However, in a head-on crash the force on the ball causes it to pull away from the magnet and turn on an electrical circuit, which starts the explosion that will create the gas for the bag.

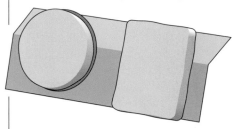

A pellet of sodium azide (NaN_3) is ignited. A rapid reaction occurs, generating nitrogen gas (N_2). This gas fills a nylon bag at a velocity of 250 to 400 km/hr. This takes only about 40 milliseconds.

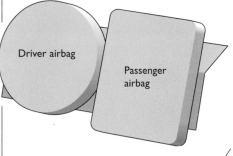

Driver airbag

Passenger airbag

When a person hits the air bag, the force of the impact is distributed over a much larger area of the body than would be the case if it hit the steering wheel or the dashboard. As a result, there are fewer severe injuries. The area that hits the air bag is shown in orange.

The force of the impact is distributed over a large area on the inflated bag.

The body of the driver or passenger should not hit the air bag while it is still inflating, or injury might occur. The air bag is designed to begin to deflate by the time the body hits it and so act as a soft cushion.

By 2 seconds after the initial impact the pressure inside the bag has reached atmospheric pressure.

Oxygen

The second gas by volume in the air is oxygen (chemical symbol O). It is a colorless, odorless, and tasteless gas.

Oxygen is very REACTIVE, meaning that it combines, or reacts, with many other elements to form COMPOUNDS. During this process it also usually gives out heat.

Oxygen is vital to all animals and to some bacteria. They take in oxygen and, in a process called RESPIRATION, use it to combine with foods to release energy for living. During this process the gas carbon dioxide is formed. It is then breathed back out to the air.

Plants absorb carbon dioxide and, by harnessing the energy from sunlight, use the carbon dioxide to make new tissues. They extract the carbon from the carbon dioxide, leaving just the oxygen, which they release into the air as oxygen gas. In this way plants and animals continually produce oxygen and carbon dioxide and recycle them in the air.

(Above) Oxygen is produced by plants through photosynthesis. The oxygen made can be seen clearly as bubbles on this aquatic plant.

(Below) The oxygen cycle.

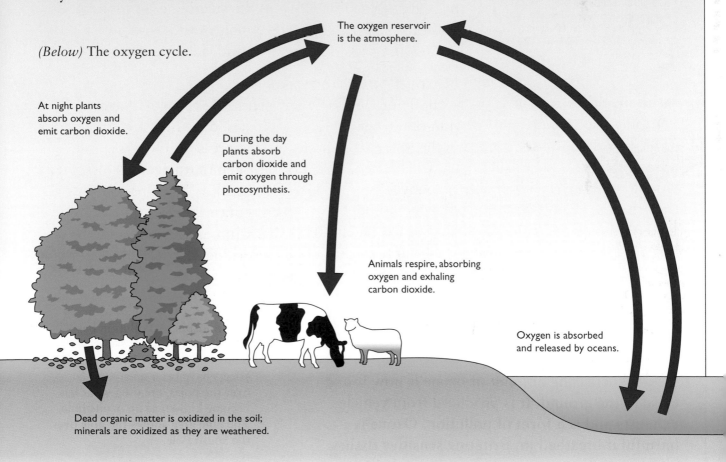

The oxygen reservoir is the atmosphere.

At night plants absorb oxygen and emit carbon dioxide.

During the day plants absorb carbon dioxide and emit oxygen through photosynthesis.

Animals respire, absorbing oxygen and exhaling carbon dioxide.

Oxygen is absorbed and released by oceans.

Dead organic matter is oxidized in the soil; minerals are oxidized as they are weathered.

Nearly all the oxygen in the air comes from growing plants. Without the oxygen released from growing plants animals and bacteria would rapidly use up the oxygen and convert it to carbon dioxide. That is why the survival of plentiful green plants in the world is literally a matter of life or death for us. Ninety percent of the oxygen produced by plants comes from the countless tiny green plants called algae that live in the world's oceans.

Oxygen and ozone

In the air oxygen consists mostly of molecules of oxygen. An oxygen molecule contains two atoms of oxygen, so oxygen in the air is given the symbol O_2. There is, however, another form of oxygen. It is made of three atoms of oxygen and so has the symbol O_3. It is called ozone.

Most ozone is found high in the atmosphere, and little occurs naturally near the ground. High in the sky the value of ozone is in its ability to absorb the Sun's ultraviolet rays, which would be harmful if too many reached the ground. The preservation of ozone in the upper atmosphere is therefore vital to life on Earth. Recently the amount of ozone has been reduced by the use of chemicals called CFCs and also by methane gas. As these gases drift into the upper atmosphere, they react with the ozone and remove it. That is why there is a worldwide attempt to reduce the use of CFCs.

An increasing amount of ozone is now found close to the ground. It is produced from vehicle exhausts and is a form of pollution. Ozone is harmful if breathed in, irritating sensitive tissues.

(Above) Satellites now continually monitor the amount of ozone in the atmosphere. Pollution has not affected the ozone content uniformly over the Earth. The effects have been most marked over the poles, creating what has become known as an ozone hole. The blue area shows the hole over the South Pole.

Where oxygen is used

Oxygen is used in large quantities in steelmaking, where it reacts with charcoal in the furnaces. It is also widely applied in the chemical industry, where it is reacted with gases that have been refined from crude oil. Acetylene, ethylene oxide, and methanol are examples of chemicals produced this way.

There is a need for oxygen in hospitals as a source of oxygen-enriched air. It is used in incubators and in life-support systems.

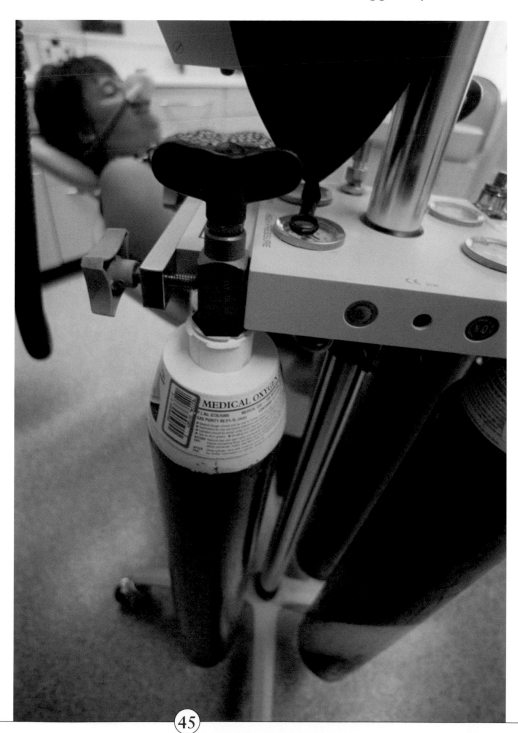

(Right) Oxygen is used in hospitals and dentists' offices.

Sulfur dioxide

A gas present in the air naturally in small amounts is sulfur dioxide. It continually cycles between the air, the oceans, and the land. Sulfur dioxide is produced during volcanic eruptions. It is partly dissolved in the oceans and partly washed out as a result of dissolving in water droplets. When sulfur dioxide dissolves in water, it produces sulfurous acid, which (together with oxides of nitrogen) is a form of acid rain.

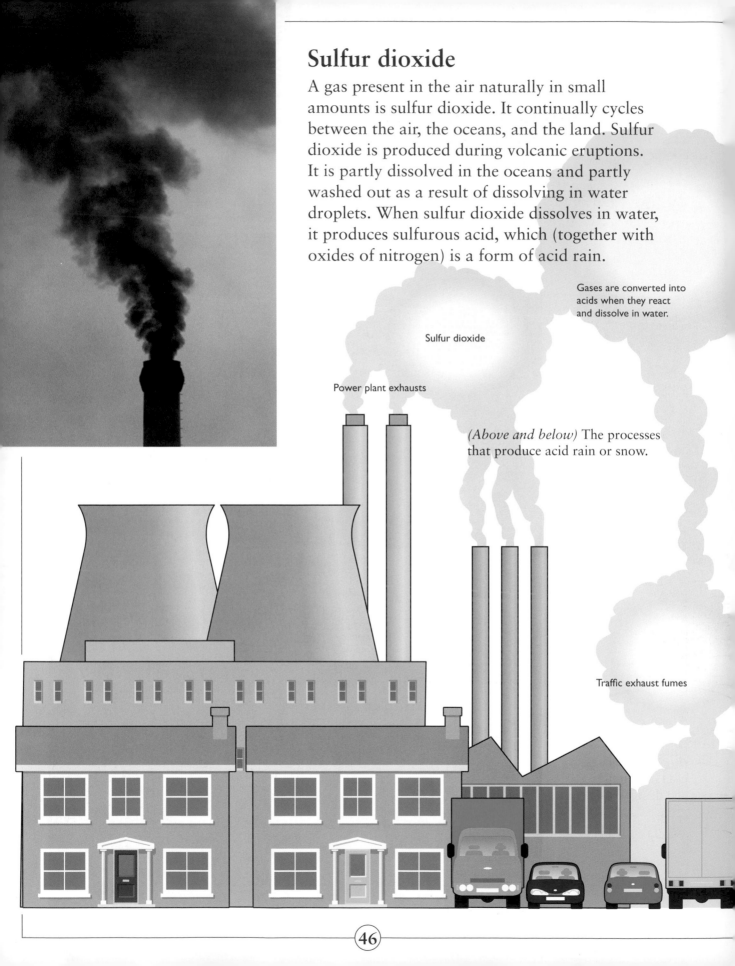

Gases are converted into acids when they react and dissolve in water.

Sulfur dioxide

Power plant exhausts

(Above and below) The processes that produce acid rain or snow.

Traffic exhaust fumes

(*Right*) Volcanic eruptions produce a natural supply of sulfur dioxide.

Sulfur gets back into the atmosphere as part of sea spray, tiny particles being thrown up into the air, which then evaporate. Some animals and bacteria also breathe out the sulfur-containing gas hydrogen sulfide. It is common in marshes and in other wetlands.

Among other acids, sulfuric acid and nitric acid are produced.

A major way in which sulfur dioxide now gets into the air, however, is from the burning of fossil fuels. Most fossil fuels contain sulfur compounds, which, when burned, combine with oxygen in the air to form sulfur dioxide. This gas is attracted to water droplets. As it dissolves in the water, it acidifies it (creating sulfurous acid). It will then fall to the ground as ACID RAIN and damage great areas of forests.

There are a number of different sources of pollution. Power plants and trash incinerators are local sources of great pollution. As a result, they can be targeted and their exhaust fumes cleaned up. Great strides in reducing sulfur dioxide have been made this way.

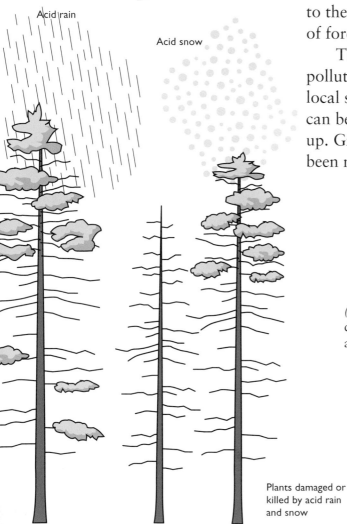

Acid rain

Acid snow

Plants damaged or killed by acid rain and snow

(*Right*) Trees damaged by acid rain.

Carbon dioxide

Carbon dioxide is colorless, tasteless, and has no smell when present in the air. As a concentrated gas, it smells slightly acidic and has a sour taste. Carbon dioxide is not a reactive gas. It will dissolve slightly in water, which is why most rainwater is naturally very slightly acidic. Over long periods of time this acid will dissolve limestone rocks, creating caves and other distinctive formations in limestone landscapes.

(Below) The carbon cycle.

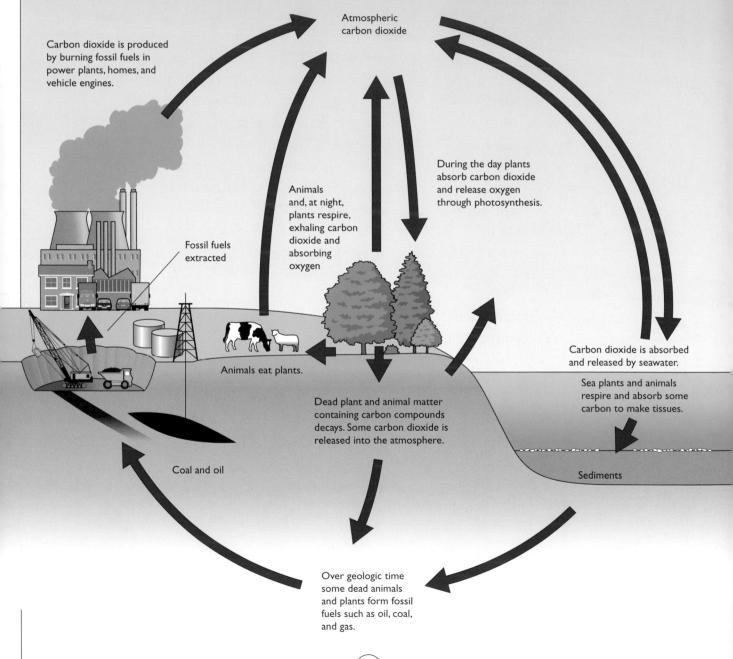

Carbon dioxide is produced by burning fossil fuels in power plants, homes, and vehicle engines.

Atmospheric carbon dioxide

During the day plants absorb carbon dioxide and release oxygen through photosynthesis.

Animals and, at night, plants respire, exhaling carbon dioxide and absorbing oxygen

Fossil fuels extracted

Animals eat plants.

Carbon dioxide is absorbed and released by seawater.

Sea plants and animals respire and absorb some carbon to make tissues.

Dead plant and animal matter containing carbon compounds decays. Some carbon dioxide is released into the atmosphere.

Coal and oil

Sediments

Over geologic time some dead animals and plants form fossil fuels such as oil, coal, and gas.

Carbon dioxide is just a minor part of the air (about 3 parts in ten thousand), but it has an extremely important role to play in our world. That is because carbon dioxide is exchanged between the air and living or dead things. It is absorbed by living plants and, in combination with the energy from sunlight, used to make tissues. It is then passed on to animals when plants are eaten. As animals digest their food and use it to make tissues and energy, carbon dioxide is released, first into the bloodstream, and then back to the air through the lungs.

When living things die, their tissue is broken down by decomposers as food, and again carbon dioxide is released back to the air. When people use plants as a fuel, carbon dioxide is also released. This all makes up the CARBON CYCLE.

When a dead organism is buried in such a way that it does not decay (as, for example, when coal- and oil-producing organisms are buried under the sea), the carbon dioxide is not released, and the tissues retain their carbon. If these materials are eventually used as fuel, the carbon is changed to carbon dioxide and released.

Over geological time the presence of plants and the burial of many of them before they could decay have resulted in a reduced amount of carbon dioxide in the air. However, since we began to burn fossil fuels, the carbon dioxide content of the air has risen again.

That is important because carbon dioxide (along with water vapor) can absorb heat radiated from the ground. As a result (and depending on the amount of carbon dioxide in the air), not all of the heat that originally reached the Earth from sunshine is returned to space. This is called the GREENHOUSE EFFECT. The current increase in carbon dioxide is about 4% every 10 years. The corresponding change in the greenhouse effect is known as GLOBAL WARMING.

Production and uses

Because it is produced when anything is burned, there is no need to try to get carbon dioxide from the air (where it is present in tiny concentrations). Instead, it is can be recovered from chimneys where it is present in high concentrations. It is also produced as a byproduct of the preparation of hydrogen.

Carbon dioxide can readily be liquefied even at normal temperatures simply by compressing it. It is commonly sold and

transported as liquid carbon dioxide. When the liquid is allowed to expand, it turns into dry ice, partly frozen snowflakelike crystals. It is used in this form for making a foglike atmosphere on the stage of theaters.

Because carbon dioxide is not a reactive gas, it is used in fire extinguishers. It is more dense than air and so settles and blankets fires, pushing the oxygen out of the way. It can also be used as a refrigerant, for making bubbles in plastics to create foams, and for inflating life rafts and life jackets. By increasing the amount of carbon dioxide in greenhouses, the gas can also be made to accelerate plant growth (just as the greenhouse effect does worldwide).

Carbon dioxide is also used to create the bubbles in fizzy drinks. Carbon dioxide is put into the drink under pressure. When the cap is released, the pressure is reduced, and the gas comes out of solution to form bubbles.

Carbon dioxide is a dangerous gas to animals because it prevents the uptake of oxygen. When people breathe shallowly, such as when they are very ill, they may not remove all of the carbon dioxide from their lungs, and that can cause death. About a 5% concentration of carbon dioxide can cause death.

Hydrogen

Hydrogen is a colorless, odorless, tasteless, but very flammable gas. Hydrogen is the most abundant element in the universe; but because it is so light, much of it is lost to space, and it only makes up a tiny part of the air.

At first, hydrogen was known as inflammable air (and as *phlogiston* by early scientists). It was first observed not in the air, where it is so rare, but by reacting an acid with a metal. Hydrogen was eventually named using the Greek words meaning "maker of water."

Because hydrogen is so light, it has an obvious use in such things as balloons. However, history proved that using an inflammable gas in a balloon is bound to lead to disaster. In 1937 the *Hindenburg*, a gigantic airship filled with hydrogen, exploded.

Hydrogen has many uses in chemistry, and it also makes an excellent rocket fuel. Because of its low concentration in the air, hydrogen cannot be obtained from air for these high-volume uses and is produced instead by chemical reactions.

(Below) Hydrogen and oxygen are mixed to produce enough force to make the rocket lift off. Hydrogen will also be used in fuel cells that will power cars by the year 2010.

Water vapor

By far the most variable of the gases in the air is water vapor. It can vary from almost nothing to 4%. Water reaches the air mostly by evaporating from oceans (although some also comes from vegetation on land, especially tropical rainforests).

Like carbon dioxide, water vapor is able to absorb heat radiated from the Earth's surface. As a result, the more water vapor in the air, the more heat is retained. Unlike carbon dioxide, however, water vapor is also able to absorb heat directly from the Sun.

When the air holds as much moisture as possible, it is said to be saturated. We measure the humidity of the air relative to this amount. As a result, the humidity of the air is called relative humidity, and it is measured in percentages. Saturated air is 100%. Except in air conditioning, outside air is normally 30% or higher.

As air cools, it can hold less moisture, and so its relative humidity climbs. Fabrics, paper, and many other materials take up moisture at higher relative humidities and go limp or stretch. Even the human hair stretches as the air gets more humid. This is, in fact, one way to measure humidity. The instrument called the hygrometer (which measures relative humidity) has a hair inside it under tension. Changes in its length cause a needle to turn in front of a dial.

The amount of water vapor that the air can hold varies with temperature. For example, at 30°C air can hold 4% water vapor. But when cooled to –40°C, the air can contain only 0.2%. A typical summer temperature for air near the ground in the tropics and subtropics is 30°C. The typical temperature for air near the upper limit of clouds is –40°C. Thus as air rises and cools, it must shed vast amounts of moisture by changing from water vapor to liquid water. This CHANGE OF STATE releases huge amounts of heat (called LATENT HEAT), which is a form of energy. It is this energy that fuels many of the most dramatic weather events, such as thunderstorms, tornadoes, and hurricanes.

The importance of humidity

High humidity has a powerful effect on many materials. For example, many fibers absorb moisture from the air. Paper becomes limp and swells when the air is damp; wood also swells, while iron begins to rust. Humidity can also affect the transmission of some types of radio waves.

Humidity is also important in some food and drink processes. In winemaking, for example, wine is

Water vapor in air

See **Vol. 8: Water** for more on water vapor.

Water droplet

Dust particle

(Above) Water vapor molecules are the cause of humidity in the lower air. When they condense onto particles of dust and salt in the air, they produce water droplets, which make cloud or fog.

first stored in wooden casks to mature. At this time air can seep into the casks. In low humidity air the alcohol of the wine becomes more concentrated, but with high humidity the wine becomes weaker.

When many people share a confined space, as for example in a school, the amount of moisture being released from each person raises the humidity of the air. Sometimes this can result in the air feeling stuffy and uncomfortable because we rely on losing moisture to stay comfortable. The more moisture there is in the air, the harder it is for water to evaporate from the skin, and so the stuffier it feels. Opening a window and allowing air to circulate is often needed (or the use of air conditioning; see page 26). But a high-humidity environment is not just uncomfortable. It is also a place where droplets of water, for example, from sneezes, do not readily evaporate. As a result, the virus microbes carried in such tiny droplets are much more easily carried between people. That is how infections such as colds are spread.

The variation in humidity also affects the weather and climate, and it also has a major influence on the way people feel. That is because the body needs to perspire, and for this it needs the air to be quite dry. As soon as the humidity of the air rises, the body cannot perspire as much, and people begin to feel sticky and sweaty. Coupled with very high temperatures, high humidity values can lead to heat stroke.

Noble gases

Noble gases is the name given to the completely unreactive, or inert, gases that make up a tiny part of the air, and whose existence was simply not known about until fairly recently. They are all colorless, odorless, and tasteless. None of them supports combustion.

There are six gases in this group, all of which are elements rather than molecules. That is, none

(Below) Balloons can be inflated with air (which produces compressed air and explains why such balloons sink in air). But they can also be filled with helium, which is much lighter than air even when compressed. You can see the difference in this picture: The helium-filled balloons are on the left and the air-filled balloons on the bottom right.

of these elements forms any kind of compound. They are helium (He), neon (Ne), argon (Ar), krypton (Kr), xenon (Xe), and radon (Rn).

Interestingly, although these gases are not very common in the air, they are not rare gases in the universe. Helium, for example, is the second most plentiful element in the universe after hydrogen. Helium is also found dissolved in oil.

Obtaining the noble gases is difficult. All except for helium and radon are produced by liquefying air. Helium is obtained from natural gas wells. Radon is produced in nuclear power plants.

Uses

The noble gases are used mainly because they do not react with other elements. They are, therefore, nonflammable. The cheapest to obtain are helium and argon, and as a result they have found the most uses.

Helium

Helium is named for the Sun (Greek = *Helios*). That is because it was first identified as a part of the Sun and only later found in the Earth's atmosphere. Air contains about five parts per million of helium.

Helium is a particularly light gas. It was probably much more common at an early stage in the Earth's history, but much of it has not been kept on the Earth by the force of gravity and has simply drifted away from the top of the atmosphere.

Helium, being so light, can be used in place of hydrogen. Helium-filled balloons, for example, are much safer than hydrogen-filled balloons.

Helium is also very poorly soluble in water and is used together with oxygen instead of nitrogen in breathing cylinders for divers. Since it does not dissolve in the blood, it does not cause the bends during rapid return to the surface.

Helium is also used to produce a noninflammable atmosphere in some places where welding and other processes using heat could cause a fire.

The boiling and freezing points of helium are lower than those of any other known substance. Helium is the only element that cannot be solidified by cooling at normal atmospheric pressure.

Argon

The most abundant of the noble gases in the air is argon. It is also the noble gas most commonly used. Argon makes up 1.3% of the atmosphere by weight and 0.94% by volume. It was the first of the noble gases to be discovered on Earth and named argon after the Greek word *argos*, meaning lazy, a comment on its inertness.

Argon slowly leaks into the air from the rocks in which it is still being formed from the decay of a rare form of potassium.

Argon can provide an atmosphere that will not burn. Its main function is to fill electric light bulbs and electronic vacuum tubes, where hot wires would burn out in air. It is also used in the production of many metals, primarily to keep oxygen away from the metal while it is being extracted from its ore. It also has an important role in providing an inert atmosphere in which silicon crystals (as in silicon chips) can be grown.

(Above) A fluorescent tube is filled with a mixture of argon and mercury vapor.

Xenon

Named for the Greek *xenos*, meaning "strange," xenon is one of the heavier gases and much rarer than other noble gases. It is four and a half times as heavy as air. Xenon occurs as one part in ten million in the air. Xenon leaks slowly from the Earth's rocks into the air.

Xenon can be used in lamps that produce a very bright, slightly blue light. Xenon flashbulbs can activate ruby lasers.

Radon

The only radioactive noble gas is radon. It is produced by the radioactive decay of radium. Radon is seven and a half times heavier than air. It is an extremely rare gas in the air and mainly found close to granite and other rocks that contain uranium.

Radium decays quite quickly and so is found in the air only over places where it is produced. However, because it is such a heavy gas, it lingers in such places and may build up in concentration.

It has been found that radon can build up in the lower rooms and basements of houses built on rocks containing uranium. As a result, radon can be breathed in. Exposure to this gas over many years can lead to a greatly increased risk of cancer. Radon is thought to be the biggest cause of lung cancer after tobacco.

Krypton

The air contains just one and a half parts of krypton in a million parts of air. The gas is named for the Greek word *kryptos*, meaning "hidden." Krypton is three times heavier than air.

Krypton is used in fluorescent lamps. One kind of krypton, krypton-85, is slightly radioactive. Leaks in air systems can be found by measuring for radioactivity at joints in piping systems.

Some car headlights now use krypton.

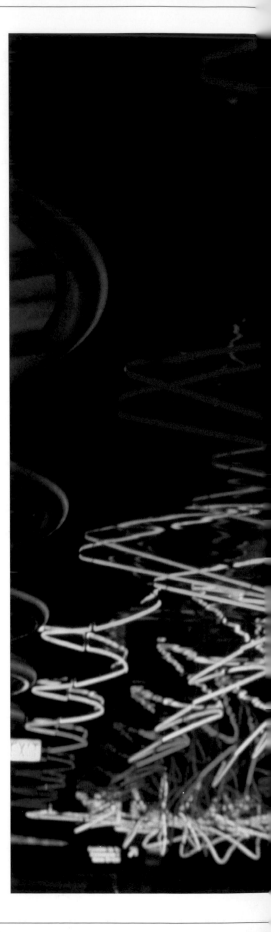

(*Right*) Neon lighting as decorative art in an airport subway.

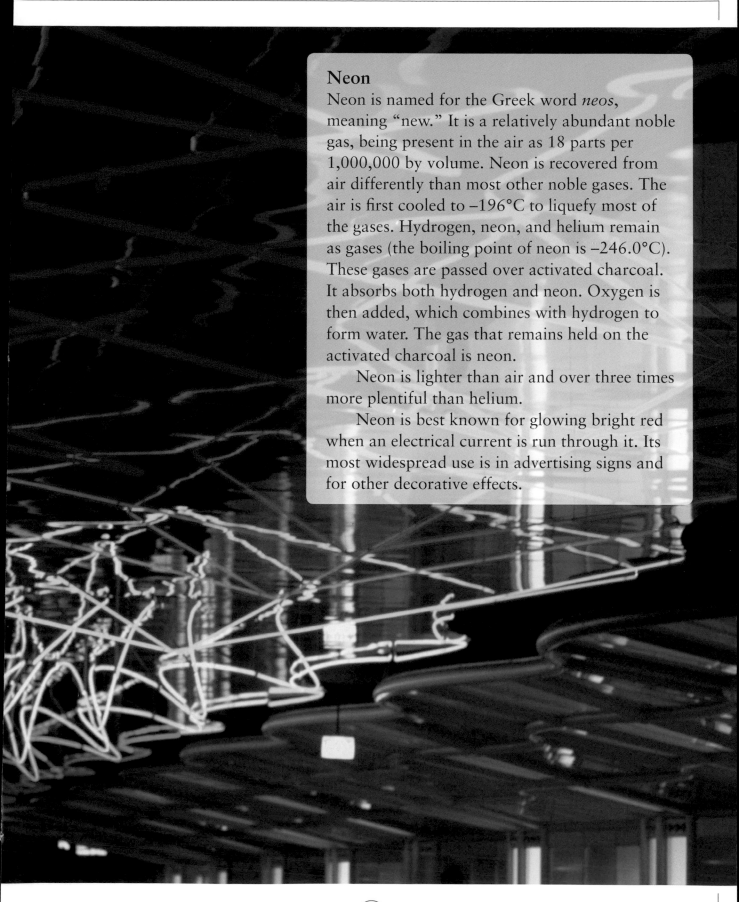

Neon

Neon is named for the Greek word *neos*, meaning "new." It is a relatively abundant noble gas, being present in the air as 18 parts per 1,000,000 by volume. Neon is recovered from air differently than most other noble gases. The air is first cooled to $-196°C$ to liquefy most of the gases. Hydrogen, neon, and helium remain as gases (the boiling point of neon is $-246.0°C$). These gases are passed over activated charcoal. It absorbs both hydrogen and neon. Oxygen is then added, which combines with hydrogen to form water. The gas that remains held on the activated charcoal is neon.

Neon is lighter than air and over three times more plentiful than helium.

Neon is best known for glowing bright red when an electrical current is run through it. Its most widespread use is in advertising signs and for other decorative effects.

Set Glossary

ACID RAIN: Rain that falls after having been contaminated by acid gases produced by power plants, vehicle exhausts, and other man-made sources.

ACIDITY: The tendency of a liquid to behave like an acid, reacting with metals and alkalis.

ADDITION POLYMERIZATION: The building blocks of many plastics (or polymers) are simple molecules called monomers. Monomers can be converted into polymers by making the monomers link to one another to form long chains in head-to-tail fashion. This is called addition polymerization or chain polymerization. It is most often used to link vinyl monomers to produce, for example, PVC, or polyvinyl chloride polymer.
See also **CONDENSATION POLYMERIZATION**

ADHESIVE: Any substance that can hold materials together simply by using some kind of surface attachment. In some cases this is a chemical reaction; in other cases it is a physical attraction between molecules of the adhesive and molecules of the substance it sticks to.

ADOBE: Simple unbaked brick made with mud, straw, and dung. It is dried in the open air. In this form it is very vulnerable to the effects of rainfall and so is most often found in desert areas or alternatively is protected by some waterproof covering, for example, thatch, straw, or reeds.

ALKALI: A base, or substance that can neutralize acids. In glassmaking an alkali is usually potassium carbonate and used as a flux to lower the melting point of the silica.

ALKYD: Any kind of synthetic resin used for protective coatings such as paint.

ALLOY: A metal mixture made up of two or more elements. Most of the elements used to make an alloy are metals. For example, brass is an alloy of copper and zinc, but carbon is an exception and used to make steel from iron.

AMALGAM: An alloy of mercury and one or more other metals. Dentist's filling amalgam traditionally contains mercury, silver, and tin.

AMPHIBIOUS: Adapted to function on both water and land.

AMORPHOUS: Shapeless and having no crystalline form. Glass is an amorphous solid.

ANION: An ion with a negative charge.

ANNEALING: A way of making a metal, alloy, or glass less brittle and more easy to work (more ductile) by heating it to a certain temperature (depending on the metal), holding it at that temperature for a certain time, and then cooling to room temperature.

ANODIZING: A method of plating metal by electrically depositing an oxide film onto the surface of a metal. The main purpose is to reduce corrosion.

ANTICYCLONE: A region of the Earth's atmosphere where the pressure is greater than average.

AQUEOUS SOLUTION: A substance dissolved in water.

ARTIFACT: An object of a previous time that was created by humans.

ARTIFICIAL DYE: A dye made from a chemical reaction that does not occur in nature. Dyes made from petroleum products are artificial dyes.

ARTIFICIAL FIBER: A fiber made from a material that has been manufactured, and that does not occur naturally. Rayon is an example of an artificial fiber.
Compare to **SYNTHETIC**

ATMOSPHERE: The envelope of gases that surrounds the Earth.

ATOM: The smallest particle of an element; a nucleus and its surrounding electrons.

AZO: A chemical compound that contains two nitrogen atoms joined by a double bond and each linked to a carbon atom. Azon compounds make up more than half of all dyes.

BARK: The exterior protective sheath of the stem and root of a woody plant such as a tree or a shrub. Everything beyond the cambium layer.

BAROMETER: An instrument for measuring atmospheric pressure.

BASE METAL: Having a low value and poorer properties than some other metals. Used, for example, when describing coins that contain metals other than gold or silver.

BAST FIBERS: A strong woody fiber that comes from the phloem of plants and is used for rope and similar products. Flax is an example of a bast fiber.

BATCH: A mixture of raw materials or products that are processes in a tank or kiln. This process produces small amounts of material or products and can be contrasted to continuous processes. Batch processing is used to make metals, alloys, glass, plastics, bricks, and other ceramics, dyes, and adhesives.

BAUXITE: A hydrated impure oxide of aluminum. It is the main ore used to obtain aluminum metal. The reddish-brown color of bauxite is caused by impurities of iron oxides.

BINDER: A substance used to make sure the pigment in a paint sticks to the surface it is applied to.

BIOCERAMICS: Ceramic materials that are used for medical and dental purposes, mainly as implants and replacements.

BLAST FURNACE: A tall furnace charged with a mixture of iron ore, coke, and limestone and used for the refining (smelting) of iron ore. The name comes from the strong blast of air used during smelting.

BLOWING: Forming a glass object by blowing into a gob of molten glass to form a bubble on the end of a blowpipe.

BOLL: The part of the cotton seed that contains the cotton fiber.

BOILING POINT: The temperature at which a liquid changes to a vapor. Boiling points change with atmospheric pressure.

BOND: A transfer or a sharing of electrons by two or more atoms. There are a number of kinds of chemical bonds, some very strong, such as covalent bonding and ionic bonding, and others quite weak, as in hydrogen bonding. Chemical bonds form because the linked molecules are more stable than the unlinked atoms from which they are formed.

BOYLE'S LAW: At constant temperature and for a given mass of gas the volume of the gas is inversely proportional to the pressure that builds up.

BRITTLE: Something that has almost no plasticity and so shatters rather than bends when a force is applied.

BULL'S EYE: A piece of glass with concentric rings marking the place where the blowpipe was attached to the glass. It is the central part of a pane of crown glass.

BUOYANCY: The tendency of an object to float if it is less dense than the liquid it is placed in.

BURN: A combustion reaction in which a flame is produced. A flame occurs where gases combust and release heat and light. At least two gases are therefore required if there is to be a flame.

CALORIFIC: Relating to the production of heat.

CAMBIUM: A thin growing layer that separates the xylem and phloem in most plants, and that produces new cell layers.

CAPACITOR: An electronic device designed for the temporary storage of electricity.

CAPILLARY ACTION, CAPILLARITY: The process by which surface tension forces can draw a liquid up a fine-bore tube.

CARBOHYDRATES: One of the main constituents of green plants, containing compounds of carbon, hydrogen, and oxygen. The main kinds of carbohydrate are sugars, starches, and celluloses.

CARBON COMPOUNDS: Any compound that includes the element carbon. Carbon compounds are also called organic compounds because they form an essential part of all living organisms.

CARBON CYCLE: The continuous movement of carbon between living things, the soil, the atmosphere, oceans, and rocks, especially those containing coal and petroleum.

CAST: To pour a liquid metal, glass, or other material into a mold and allow it to cool so that it solidifies and takes on the shape of the mold.

CATALYST: A substance that speeds up a chemical reaction but itself remains unchanged. For example, platinum is used in a catalytic converter of gases in the exhausts leaving motor vehicles.

CATALYTIC EFFECT: The way a substance helps speed up a reaction even though that substance does not form part of the reaction.

CATHODIC PROTECTION: The technique of protecting a metal object by connecting it to a more easily oxidizable material. The metal object being protected is made into the cathode of a cell. For example, iron can be protected by coupling it with magnesium.

CATION: An ion with a positive charge, often a metal.

CELL: A vessel containing two electrodes and a liquid substance that conducts electricity (an electrolyte).

CELLULOSE: A form of carbohydrate. *See* **CARBOHYDRATE**

CEMENT: A mixture of alumina, silica, lime, iron oxide, and magnesium oxide that is burned together in a kiln and then made into a powder. It is used as the main ingredient of mortar and as the adhesive in concrete.

CERAMIC: A crystalline nonmetal. In a more everyday sense it is a material based on clay that has been heated so that it has chemically hardened.

CHARRING: To burn partly so that some of a material turns to carbon and turns black.

CHINA: A shortened version of the original "Chinese porcelain," it also refers to various porcelain objects such as plates and vases meant for domestic use.

CHINA CLAY: The mineral kaolinite, which is a very white clay used as the basis of porcelain manufacture.

CLAY MINERALS: The minerals, such as kaolinite, illite, and montmorillonite, that occur naturally in soils and some rocks, and that are all minute platelike crystals.

COKE: A form of coal that has been roasted in the absence of air to remove much of the liquid and gas content.

COLORANTS: Any substance that adds a color to a material. The pigments in paints and the chemicals that make dyes are colorants.

COLORFAST: A dye that will not "run" in water or change color when it is exposed to sunlight.

COMPOSITE MATERIALS: Materials such as plywood that are normally regarded as a single material, but that themselves are made up of a number of different materials bonded together.

COMPOUND: A chemical consisting of two or more elements chemically bonded together, for example, calcium carbonate.

COMPRESSED AIR: Air that has been squashed to reduce its volume.

COMPRESSION: To be squashed.

COMPRESSION MOLDING: The shaping of an object, such as a headlight lens, which is achieved by squashing it into a mold.

CONCRETE: A mixture of cement and a coarse material such as sand and small stones.

CONDENSATION: The process of changing a gas to a liquid.

CONDENSATION POLYMERIZATION: The production of a polymer formed by a chain of reactions in which a water molecule is eliminated as every link of the polymer is formed. Polyester is an example.

CONDUCTION: (i) The exchange of heat (heat conduction) by contact with another object, or (ii) allowing the flow of electrons (electrical conduction).

CONDUCTIVITY: The property of allowing the flow of heat or electricity.

CONDUCTOR: (i) Heat—a material that allows heat to flow in and out of it easily. (ii) Electricity—a material that allows electrons to flow through it easily.

CONTACT ADHESIVE: An adhesive that, when placed on the surface to be joined, sticks as soon as the surfaces are placed firmly together.

CONVECTION: The circulating movement of molecules in a liquid or gas as a result of heating it from below.

CORRODE/CORROSION: A reaction usually between a metal and an acid or alkali in which the metal decomposes. The word is used in the sense of the metal being eaten away and dangerously thinned.

CORROSIVE: Causing corrosion, that is, the oxidation of a metal. For example, sodium hydroxide is corrosive.

COVALENT BONDING: The most common type of strong chemical bond, which occurs when two atoms share electrons. For example, oxygen O_2.

CRANKSHAFT: A rodlike piece of a machine designed to change linear into rotational motion or vice versa.

CRIMP: To cause to become wavy.

CRUCIBLE: A ceramic-lined container for holding molten metal, glass, and so on.

CRUDE OIL: A chemical mixture of petroleum liquids. Crude oil forms the raw material for an oil refinery.

CRYSTAL: A substance that has grown freely so that it can develop external faces.

CRYSTALLINE: A solid in which the atoms, ions, or molecules are organized into an orderly pattern without distinct crystal faces.

CURING: The process of allowing a chemical change to occur simply by waiting a while. Curing is often a process of reaction with water or with air.

CYLINDER GLASS: An old method of making window glass by blowing a large bubble of glass, then swinging it until it forms a cylinder. The ends of the cylinder are then cut off with shears and the sides of the cylinder allowed to open out until they form a flat sheet.

DECIDUOUS: A plant that sheds its leaves seasonally.

DECOMPOSE: To rot. Decomposing plant matter releases nutrients back to the soil and in this way provides nourishment for a new generation of living things.

DENSITY: The mass per unit volume (for example, g/c^3).

DESICCATE: To dry up thoroughly.

DETERGENT: A cleaning agent that is able to turn oils and dirts into an emulsion and then hold them in suspension so they can be washed away.

DIE: A tool for giving metal a required shape either by striking the object with the die or by forcing the object over or through the die.

DIFFUSION: The slow mixing of one substance with another until the two substances are evenly mixed. Mixing occurs because of differences in concentration within the mixture. Diffusion works rapidly with gases, very slowly with liquids.

DILUTE: To add more of a solvent to a solution.

DISSOCIATE: To break up. When a compound dissociates, its molecules break up into separate ions.

DISSOLVED: To break down a substance in a solution without causing a reaction.

DISTILLATION: The process of separating mixtures by condensing the vapors through cooling. The simplest form of distillation uses a Liebig condenser arranged with just a slight slope down to the collecting vessel. When the liquid mixture is heated and vapors are produced, they enter the water cooled condenser and then flow down the tube, where they can be collected.

DISTILLED WATER: Water that has its dissolved solids removed by the process of distillation.

DOPING: Adding an impurity to the surface of a substance in order to change its properties.

DORMANT: A period of inactivity such as during winter, when plants stop growing.

DRAWING: The process in which a piece of metal is pulled over a former or through dies.

DRY-CLEANED: A method of cleaning fabrics with nonwater-based organic solvents such as carbon tetrachloride.

DUCTILE: Capable of being drawn out or hammered thin.

DYE: A colored substance that will stick to another substance so that both appear to be colored.

EARLY WOOD: The wood growth put on the spring of each year.

EARTHENWARE: Pottery that has not been fired to the point where some of the clay crystals begin to melt and fuse together and is thus slightly porous and coarser than stoneware or porcelain.

ELASTIC: The ability of an object to regain its original shape after it has been deformed.

ELASTIC CHANGE: To change shape elastically.

ELASTICITY: The property of a substance that causes it to return to its original shape after it has been deformed in some way.

ELASTIC LIMIT: The largest force that a material can stand before it changes shape permanently.

ELECTRODE: A conductor that forms one terminal of a cell.

ELECTROLYSIS: An electrical-chemical process that uses an electric current to cause the breakup of a compound and the movement of metal ions in a solution. It is commonly used in industry for purifying (refining) metals or for plating metal objects with a fine, even metal coat.

ELECTROLYTE: An ionic solution that conducts electricity.

ELECTROMAGNET: A temporary magnet that is produced when a current of electricity passes through a coil of wire.

ELECTRON: A tiny, negatively charged particle that is part of an atom. The flow of electrons through a solid material such as a wire produces an electric current.

ELEMENT: A substance that cannot be decomposed into simpler substances by chemical means, for example, silver and copper.

EMULSION: Tiny droplets of one substance dispersed in another.

EMULSION PAINT: A paint made of an emulsion that is water soluble (also called latex paint).

ENAMEL: A substance made of finely powdered glass colored with a metallic oxide and suspended in oil so that it can be applied with a brush. The enamel is then heated, the oil burns away, and the glass fuses. Also used colloquially to refer to certain kinds of resin-based paint that have extremely durable properties.

ENGINEERED WOOD PRODUCTS: Wood products such as plywood sheeting made from a combination of wood sheets, chips or sawdust, and resin.

EVAPORATION: The change of state of a liquid to a gas. Evaporation happens below the boiling point.

EXOTHERMIC REACTION: A chemical reaction that gives out heat.

EXTRUSION: To push a substance through an opening so as to change its shape.

FABRIC: A material made by weaving threads into a network, often just referred to as cloth.

FELTED: Wool that has been hammered in the presence of heat and moisture to change its texture and mat the fibers.

FERRITE: A magnetic substance made of ferric oxide combined with manganese, nickel, or zinc oxide.

FIBER: A long thread.

FILAMENT: (i) The coiled wire used inside a light bulb. It consists of a high-resistance metal such as tungsten that also has a high melting point. (ii) A continuous thread produced during the manufacture of fibers.

FILLER: A material introduced in order to give bulk to a substance. Fillers are used in making paper and also in the manufacture of paints and some adhesives.

FILTRATE: The liquid that has passed through a filter.

FLOOD: When rivers spill over their banks and cover the surrounding land with water.

FLUID: Able to flow either as a liquid or a gas.

FLUORESCENT: A substance that gives out visible light when struck by invisible waves, such as ultraviolet rays.

FLUX: A substance that lowers the melting temperature of another substance. Fluxes are use in glassmaking and in melting alloys. A flux is used, for example, with a solder.

FORMER: An object used to control the shape or size of a product being made, for example, glass.

FOAM: A material that is sufficiently gelatinous to be able to contain bubbles of gas. The gas bulks up the substances, making it behave as though it were semirigid.

FORGE: To hammer a piece of heated metal until it changes to the desired shape.

FRACTION: A group of similar components of a mixture. In the petroleum industry the light fractions of crude oil are those with the smallest molecules, while the medium and heavy fractions have larger molecules.

FRACTIONAL DISTILLATION: The separation of the components of a liquid mixture by heating them to their boiling points.

FREEZING POINT: The temperature at which a substance undergoes a phase change from a liquid to a solid. It is the same temperature as the melting point.

FRIT: Partly fused materials of which glass is made.

FROTH SEPARATION: A process in which air bubbles are blown through a suspension, causing a froth of bubbles to collect on the surface. The materials that are attracted to the bubbles can then be removed with the froth.

FURNACE: An enclosed fire designed to produce a very high degree of heat for melting glass or metal or for reheating objects so they can be further processed.

FUSING: The process of melting particles of a material so they form a continuous sheet or solid object. Enamel is bonded to the surface of glass this way. Powder-formed metal is also fused into a solid piece. Powder paints are fused to the surface by heating.

GALVANIZING: The application of a surface coating of zinc to iron or steel.

GAS: A form of matter in which the molecules take no definite shape and are free to move around to uniformly fill any vessel they are put in. A gas can easily be compressed into a much smaller volume.

GIANT MOLECULES: Molecules that have been formed by polymerization.

GLASS: A homogeneous, often transparent material with a random noncrystalline molecular structure. It is achieved by cooling a molten substance very rapidly so that it cannot crystallize.

GLASS CERAMIC: A ceramic that is not entirely crystalline.

GLASSY STATE: A solid in which the molecules are arranged randomly rather than being formed into crystals.

GLOBAL WARMING: The progressive increase in the average temperature of the Earth's atmosphere, most probably in large part due to burning fossil fuels.

GLUE: An adhesive made from boiled animal bones.

GOB: A piece of near-molten glass used by glass-blowers and in machines to make hollow glass vessels.

GRAIN: (i) The distinctive pattern of fibers in wood. (ii) Small particles of a solid, including a single crystal.

GRAPHITE: A form of the element carbon with a sheetlike structure.

GRAVITY: The attractive force produced because of the mass of an object.

GREENHOUSE EFFECT: An increase in the global air temperature as a result of heat released from burning fossil fuels being absorbed by carbon dioxide in the atmosphere.

GREENHOUSE GAS: Any of various gases that contribute to the greenhouse effect, such as carbon dioxide.

GROUNDWATER: Water that flows naturally through rocks as part of the water cycle.

GUM: Any natural adhesive of plant origin that consists of colloidal polysaccharide substances that are gelatinous when moist but harden on drying.

HARDWOOD: The wood from a nonconiferous tree.

HEARTWOOD: The old, hard, nonliving central wood of trees.

HEAT: The energy that is transferred when a substance is at a different temperature than that of its surroundings.

HEAT CAPACITY: The ratio of the heat supplied to a substance compared with the rise in temperature that is produced.

HOLOGRAM: A three-dimensional image reproduced from a split laser beam.

HYDRATION: The process of absorption of water by a substance. In some cases hydration makes a substance change color, but in all cases there is a change in volume.

HYDROCARBON: A compound in which only hydrogen and carbon atoms are present. Most fuels are hydrocarbons, for example, methane.

HYDROFLUORIC ACID: An extremely corrosive acid that attacks silicate minerals such as glass. It is used to etch decoration onto glass and also to produce some forms of polished surface.

HYDROGEN BOND: A type of attractive force that holds one molecule to another. It is one of the weaker forms of intermolecular attractive force.

HYDROLYSIS: A reversible process of decomposition of a substance in water.

HYDROPHILIC: Attracted to water.

HYDROPHOBIC: Repelled by water.

IMMISCIBLE: Will not mix with another substance, for example, oil and water.

IMPURITIES: Any substances that are found in small quantities, and that are not meant to be in the solution or mixture.

INCANDESCENT: Glowing with heat, for example, a tungsten filament in a light bulb.

INDUSTRIAL REVOLUTION: The time, which began in the 18th century and continued through into the 19th century, when materials began to be made with the use of power machines and mass production.

INERT: A material that does not react chemically.

INORGANIC: A substance that does not contain the element carbon (and usually hydrogen), for example, sodium chloride.

INSOLUBLE: A substance that will not dissolve, for example, gold in water.

INSULATOR: A material that does not conduct electricity.

ION: An atom or group of atoms that has gained or lost one or more electrons and so developed an electrical charge.

IONIC BONDING: The form of bonding that occurs between two ions when the ions have opposite charges, for example, sodium ions bond with chloride ions to make sodium chloride. Ionic bonds are strong except in the presence of a solvent.

IONIZE: To change into ions.

ISOTOPE: An atom that has the same number of protons in its nucleus, but that has a different mass, for example, carbon 12 and carbon 14.

KAOLINITE: A form of clay mineral found concentrated as china clay. It is the result of the decomposition of the mineral feldspar.

KILN: An oven used to heat materials. Kilns at quite low temperatures are used to dry wood and at higher temperatures to bake bricks and to fuse enamel onto the surfaces of other substances. They are a form of furnace.

KINETIC ENERGY: The energy due to movement. When a ball is thrown, it has kinetic energy.

KNOT: The changed pattern in rings in wood due to the former presence of a branch.

LAMINATE: An engineered wood product consisting of several wood layers bonded by a resin. Also applies to strips of paper stuck together with resins to make such things as "formica" worktops.

LATE WOOD: Wood produced during the summer part of the growing season.

LATENT HEAT: The amount of heat that is absorbed or released during the process of changing state between gas, liquid, or solid. For example, heat is absorbed when liquid changes to gas. Heat is given out again as the gas condenses back to a liquid.

LATEX: A general term for a colloidal suspension of rubber-type material in water. Originally for the milky white liquid emulsion found in the Para rubber tree, but also now any manufactured water emulsion containing synthetic rubber or plastic.

LATEX PAINT: A water emulsion of a synthetic rubber or plastic used as paint. *See* EMULSION PAINT

LATHE: A tool consisting of a rotating spindle and cutters that is designed to produce shaped objects that are symmetrical about the axis of rotation.

LATTICE: A regular geometric arrangement of objects in space.

LEHR: The oven used for annealing glassware. It is usually a very long tunnel through which glass passes on a conveyor belt.

LIGHTFAST: A colorant that does not fade when exposed to sunlight.

LIGNIN: A form of hard cellulose that forms the walls of cells.

LIQUID: A form of matter that has a fixed volume but no fixed shape.

LUMBER: Timber that has been dressed for use in building or carpentry and consists of planed planks.

MALLEABLE: Capable of being hammered or rolled into a new shape without fracturing due to brittleness.

MANOMETER: A device for measuring liquid or gas pressure.

MASS: The amount of matter in an object. In common use the word weight is used instead (incorrectly) to mean mass.

MATERIAL: Anything made of matter.

MATTED: Another word for felted. *See* FELTED

MATTER: Anything that has mass and takes up space.

MELT: The liquid glass produced when a batch of raw materials melts. Also used to describe molten metal.

MELTING POINT: The temperature at which a substance changes state from a solid phase to a liquid phase. It is the same as the freezing point.

METAL: A class of elements that is a good conductor of electricity and heat, has a metallic luster, is malleable and ductile, and is formed as cations held together by a sea of electrons. A metal may also be an alloy of these elements and carbon.

METAL FATIGUE: The gradual weakening of a metal by constant bending until a crack develops.

MINERAL: A solid substance made of just one element or compound, for example, calcite minerals contain only calcium carbonate.

MISCIBLE: Capable of being mixed.

MIXTURE: A material that can be separated into two or more substances using physical means, for example, air.

MOLD: A containing shape made of wood, metal, or sand into which molten glass or metal is poured. In metalworking it produces a casting. In glassmaking the glass is often blown rather than poured when making, for example, light bulbs.

MOLECULE: A group of two or more atoms held together by chemical bonds.

MONOMER: A small molecule and building block for larger chain molecules or polymers (mono means "one" and mer means "part").

MORDANT: A chemical that is attracted to a dye and also to the surface that is to be dyed.

MOSAIC: A decorated surface made from a large number of small colored pieces of glass, natural stone, or ceramic that are cemented together.

NATIVE METAL: A pure form of a metal not combined as a compound. Native metals are more common in nonreactive elements such as gold than reactive ones such as calcium.

NATURAL DYES: Dyes made from plants without any chemical alteration, for example, indigo.

NATURAL FIBERS: Fibers obtained from plants or animals, for example, flax and wool.

NEUTRON: A particle inside the nucleus of an atom that is neutral and has no charge.

NOBLE GASES: The members of group 8 of the periodic table of the elements: helium, neon, argon, krypton, xenon, radon. These gases are almost entirely unreactive.

NONMETAL: A brittle substance that does not conduct electricity, for example, sulfur or nitrogen.

OIL-BASED PAINTS: Paints that are not based on water as a vehicle. Traditional artists' oil paint uses linseed oil as a vehicle.

OPAQUE: A substance through which light cannot pass.

ORE: A rock containing enough of a useful substance to make mining it worthwhile, for example, bauxite, the ore of aluminum.

ORGANIC: A substance that contains carbon and usually hydrogen. The carbonates are usually excluded.

OXIDE: A compound that includes oxygen and one other element, for example, Cu_2O, copper oxide.

OXIDIZE, OXIDIZING AGENT: A reaction that occurs when a substance combines with oxygen or a reaction in which an atom, ion, or molecule loses electrons to another substance (and in this more general case does not have to take up oxygen).

OZONE: A form of oxygen whose molecules contain three atoms of oxygen. Ozone high in the atmosphere blocks harmful ultraviolet rays from the Sun, but at ground level it is an irritant gas when breathed in and so is regarded as a form of pollution. The ozone layer is the uppermost part of the stratosphere.

PAINT: A coating that has both decorative and protective properties, and that consists of a pigment suspended in a vehicle, or binder, made of a resin dissolved in a solvent. It dries to give a tough film.

PARTIAL PRESSURE: The pressure a gas in a mixture would exert if it alone occupied the flask. For example, oxygen makes up about a fifth of the atmosphere. Its partial pressure is therefore about a fifth of normal atmospheric pressure.

PASTE: A thick suspension of a solid in a liquid.

PATINA: A surface coating that develops on metals and protects them from further corrosion, for example, the green coating of copper carbonate that forms on copper statues.

PERIODIC TABLE: A chart organizing elements by atomic number and chemical properties into groups and periods.

PERMANENT HARDNESS: Hardness in the water that cannot be removed by boiling.

PETROCHEMICAL: Any of a large group of manufactured chemicals (not fuels) that come from petroleum and natural gas. It is usually taken to include similar products that can be made from coal and plants.

PETROLEUM: A natural mixture of a range of gases, liquids, and solids derived from the decomposed remains of animals and plants.

PHASE: A particular state of matter. A substance can exist as a solid, liquid, or gas and may change between these phases with the addition or removal of energy, usually in the form of heat.

PHOSPHOR: A material that glows when energized by ultraviolet or electron beams, such as in fluorescent tubes and cathode ray tubes.

PHOTOCHEMICAL SMOG: A mixture of tiny particles of dust and soot combined with a brown haze caused by the reaction of colorless nitric oxide from vehicle exhausts and oxygen of the air to form brown nitrogen dioxide.

PHOTOCHROMIC GLASSES: Glasses designed to change color with the intensity of light. They use the property that certain substances, for example, silver halide, can change color (and change chemically) in light. For example, when silver chromide is dispersed in the glass melt, sunlight decomposes the silver halide to release silver (and so darken the lens). But the halogen cannot escape; and when the light is removed, the halogen recombines with the silver to turn back to colorless silver halide.

PHOTOSYNTHESIS: The natural process that happens in green plants whereby the energy from light is used to help turn gases, water, and minerals into tissue and energy.

PIEZOELECTRICS: Materials that produce electric currents when they are deformed, or vice versa.

PIGMENT: Insoluble particles of coloring material.

PITH: The central strand of spongy tissue found in the stems of most plants.

PLASTIC: Material—a carbon-based substance consisting of long chains or networks (polymers) of simple molecules. The word plastic is commonly used only for synthetic polymers. Property—a material is plastic if it can be made to change shape easily and then remain in this new shape (contrast with elasticity and brittleness).

PLASTIC CHANGE: A permanent change in shape that happens without breaking.

PLASTICIZER: A chemical added to rubbers and resins to make it easier for them to be deformed and molded. Plasticizers are also added to cement to make it more easily worked when used as a mortar.

PLATE GLASS: Rolled, ground, and polished sheet glass.

PLIABLE: Supple enough to be repeatedly bent without fracturing.

PLYWOOD: An engineered wood laminate consisting of sheets of wood bonded with resin. Each sheet of wood has the grain at right angles to the one above and below. This imparts stability to the product.

PNEUMATIC DEVICE: Any device that works with air pressure.

POLAR: Something that has a partial electric charge.

POLYAMIDES: A compound that contains more than one amide group, for example, nylon.

POLYMER: A compound that is made of long chains or branching networks by combining molecules called monomers as repeating units. Poly means "many," mer means "part."

PORCELAIN: A hard, fine-grained, and translucent white ceramic that is made of china clay and is fired to a high temperature. Varieties include china.

PORES: Spaces between particles that are small enough to hold water by capillary action, but large enough to allow water to enter.

POROUS: A material that has small cavities in it, known as pores. These pores may or may not be joined. As a result, porous materials may or may not allow a liquid or gas to pass through them. Popularly, porous is used to mean permeable, the kind of porosity in which the pores are joined, and liquids or gases can flow.

POROUS CERAMICS: Ceramics that have not been fired at temperatures high enough to cause the clays to fuse and so prevent the slow movement of water.

POTENTIAL ENERGY: Energy due to the position of an object. Water in a reservoir has potential energy because it is stored up, and when released, it moves down to a lower level.

POWDER COATING: The application of a pigment in powder form without the use of a solvent.

POWDER FORMING: A process of using a powder to fill a mold and then heating the powder to make it fuse into a solid.

PRECIPITATE: A solid substance formed as a result of a chemical reaction between two liquids or gases.

PRESSURE: The force per unit area measured in SI units in Pascals and also more generally in atmospheres.

PRIMARY COLORS: A set of colors from which all others can be made. In transmitted light they are red, blue, and green.

PROTEIN: Substances in plants and animals that include nitrogen.

PROTON: A positively charged particle in the nucleus of an atom that balances out the charge of the surrounding electrons.

QUENCH: To put into water in order to cool rapidly.

RADIATION: The transmission of energy from one body to another without any contribution from the intervening space. *Contrast with* **CONVECTION** and **CONDUCTION**

RADIOACTIVE: A substance that spontaneously emits energetic particles.

RARE EARTHS: Any of a group of metal oxides that are found widely throughout the Earth's rocks, but in low concentrations. They are mainly made up of the elements of the lanthanide series of the periodic table of the elements.

RAW MATERIAL: A substance that has not been prepared, but that has an intended use in manufacturing.

RAY: Narrow beam of light.

RAYON: An artificial fiber made from natural cellulose.

REACTION (CHEMICAL): The recombination of two substances using parts of each substance.

REACTIVE: A substance that easily reacts with many other substances.

RECYCLE: To take once used materials and make them available for reuse.

REDUCTION, REDUCING AGENT: The removal of oxygen from or the addition of hydrogen to a compound.

REFINING: Separating a mixture into the simpler substances of which it is made, especially petrochemical refining.

REFRACTION: The bending of a ray of light as it passes between substances of different refractive index (light-bending properties).

REFRACTORY: Relating to the use of a ceramic material, especially a brick, in high-temperature conditions of, for example, a furnace.

REFRIGERANT: A substance that, on changing between a liquid and a gas, can absorb large amounts of (latent) heat from its surroundings.

REGENERATED FIBERS: Fibers that have been dissolved in a solution and then recovered from the solution in a different form.

REINFORCED FIBER: A fiber that is mixed with a resin, for example, glass-reinforced fiber.

RESIN: A semisolid natural material that is made of plant secretions and often yellow-brown in color. Also synthetic

materials with the same type of properties. Synthetic resins have taken over almost completely from natural resins and are available as thermoplastic resins and thermosetting resins.

RESPIRATION: The process of taking in oxygen and releasing carbon dioxide in animals and the reverse in plants.

RIVET: A small rod of metal that is inserted into two holes in metal sheets and then burred over at both ends in order to stick the sheets together.

ROCK: A naturally hard inorganic material composed of mineral particles or crystals.

ROLLING: The process in which metal is rolled into plates and bars.

ROSIN: A brittle form of resin used in varnishes.

RUST: The product of the corrosion of iron and steel in the presence of air and water.

SALT: Generally thought of as sodium chloride, common salt; however, more generally a salt is a compound involving a metal. There are therefore many "salts" in water in addition to sodium chloride.

SAPWOOD: The outer, living layers of the tree, which includes cells for the transportation of water and minerals between roots and leaves.

SATURATED: A state in which a liquid can hold no more of a substance dissolved in it.

SEALANTS: A material designed to stop water or other liquids from penetrating into a surface or between surfaces. Most sealants are adhesives.

SEMICONDUCTOR: A crystalline solid that has an electrical conductivity part way between a conductor and an insulator. This material can be altered by doping to control an electric current. Semiconductors are the basis of transistors, integrated circuits, and other modern electronic solid-state devices.

SEMIPERMEABLE MEMBRANE: A thin material that acts as a fine sieve or filter, allowing small molecules to pass, but holding back large molecules.

SEPARATING COLUMN: A tall glass tube containing a porous disk near the base and filled with a substance such as aluminum oxide that can absorb materials on its surface. When a mixture passes through the columns, fractions are retarded by differing amounts so that each fraction is washed through the column in sequence.

SEPARATING FUNNEL: A pear-shaped glass funnel designed to permit the separation of immiscible liquids by simply pouring off the more dense liquid from the bottom of the funnel, while leaving the less dense liquid in the funnel.

SHAKES: A defect in wood produced by the wood tissue separating, usually parallel to the rings.

SHEEN: A lustrous, shiny surface on a yarn. It is produced by the finishing process or may be a natural part of the yarn.

SHEET-METAL FORMING: The process of rolling out metal into sheet.

SILICA: Silicon dioxide, most commonly in the form of sand.

SILICA GLASS: Glass made exclusively of silica.

SINTER: The process of heating that makes grains of a ceramic or metal a solid mass before it becomes molten.

SIZE: A glue, varnish, resin, or similar very dilute adhesive sealant used to block up the pores in porous surfaces or, for example, plaster and paper. Once the size has dried, paint or other surface coatings can be applied without the coating sinking in.

SLAG: A mixture of substances that are waste products of a furnace. Most slag are mainly composed of silicates.

SMELTING: Roasting a substance in order to extract the metal contained in it.

SODA: A flux for glassmaking consisting of sodium carbonate.

SOFTWOOD: Wood obtained from a coniferous tree.

SOLID: A rigid form of matter that maintains its shape regardless of whether or not it is in a container.

SOLIDIFICATION: Changing from a liquid to a solid.

SOLUBILITY: The maximum amount of a substance that can be contained in a solvent.

SOLUBLE: Readily dissolvable in a solvent.

SOLUTION: A mixture of a liquid (the solvent) and at least one other substance of lesser abundance (the solute). Like all mixtures, solutions can be separated by physical means.

SOLVAY PROCESS: Modern method of manufacturing the industrial alkali sodium carbonate (soda ash).

SOLVENT: The main substance in a solution.

SPECTRUM: A progressive series arranged in order, for example, the range of colors that make up visible light as seen in a rainbow.

SPINNERET: A small metal nozzle perforated with many small holes through which a filament solution is forced. The filaments that emerge are solidified by cooling and the filaments twisted together to form a yarn.

SPINNING: The process of drawing out and twisting short fibers, for example, wool, and thus making a thread or yarn.

SPRING: A natural flow of water from the ground.

STABILIZER: A chemical that, when added to other chemicals, prevents further reactions. For example, in soda lime glass the lime acts as a stabilizer for the silica.

STAPLE: A short fiber that has to be twisted with other fibers (spun) in order to make a long thread or yarn.

STARCHES: One form of carbohydrate. Starches can be used to make adhesives.

STATE OF MATTER: The physical form of matter. There are three states of matter: liquid, solid, and gas.

STEAM: Water vapor at the boiling point of water.

STONEWARE: Nonwhite pottery that has been fired at a high temperature until some of the clay has fused, a state called vitrified. Vitrification makes the pottery impervious to water. It is used for general tableware, often for breakfast crockery.

STRAND: When a number of yarns are twisted together, they make a strand. Strands twisted together make a rope.

SUBSTANCE: A type of material including mixtures.

SULFIDE: A compound that is composed only of metal and sulfur atoms, for example, PbS, the mineral galena.

SUPERCONDUCTORS: Materials that will conduct electricity with virtually no resistance if they are cooled to temperatures close to absolute zero (−273°C).

SURFACE TENSION: The force that operates on the surface of a liquid, and that makes it act as though it were covered with an invisible elastic film.

SURFACTANT: A substance that acts on a surface, such as a detergent.

SUSPENDED, SUSPENSION: Tiny particles in a liquid or a gas that do not settle out with time.

SYNTHETIC: Something that does not occur naturally but has to be manufactured. Synthetics are often produced from materials that do not occur in nature, for example, from petrochemicals. (i) Dye—a synthetic dye is made from petrochemicals, as opposed to natural dyes that are made of extracts of plants. (ii) Fiber—synthetic is a subdivision of artificial. Although both polyester and rayon are artificial fibers, rayon is made from reconstituted natural cellulose fibers and so is not synthetic, while polyester is made from petrochemicals and so is a synthetic fiber.

TANNIN: A group of pale-yellow or light-brown substances derived from plants that are used in dyeing fabric and making ink. Tannins are soluble in water and produce dark-blue or dark-green solutions when added to iron compounds.

TARNISH: A coating that develops as a result of the reaction between a metal and the substances in the air. The most common form of tarnishing is a very thin transparent oxide coating, such as occurs on aluminum. Sulfur compounds in the air make silver tarnish black.

TEMPER: To moderate or to make stronger: used in the metal industry to describe softening hardened steel or cast iron by reheating at a lower temperature or to describe hardening steel by reheating and cooling in oil; or in the glass industry, to describe toughening glass by first heating it and then slowly cooling it.

TEMPORARILY HARD WATER: Hard water that contains dissolved substances that can be removed by boiling.

TENSILE (PULLING STRENGTH): The greatest lengthwise (pulling) stress a substance can bear without tearing apart.

TENSION: A state of being pulled. Compare to compression.

TERRA COTTA: Red earth-colored glazed or unglazed fired clay whose origins lie in the Mediterranean region of Europe.

THERMOPLASTIC: A plastic that will soften and can be molded repeatedly into different shapes. It will then set into the molded shape as it cools.

THERMOSET: A plastic that will set into a molded shape as it first cools, but that cannot be made soft again by reheating.

THREAD: A long length of filament, group of filaments twisted together, or a long length of short fibers that have been spun and twisted together into a continuous strand.

TIMBER: A general term for wood suitable for building or for carpentry and consisting of roughcut planks.
Compare to **LUMBER**

TRANSITION METALS: Any of the group of metallic elements (for example, chromium and iron) that belong to the central part of the periodic table of the elements and whose oxides commonly occur in a variety of colors.

TRANSPARENT: Something that will readily let light through, for example, window glass. Compare to translucent, when only some light gets through but an image cannot be seen, for example, greaseproof paper.

TROPOSPHERE: The lower part of the atmosphere in which clouds form. In general, temperature decreases with height.

TRUNK: The main stem of a tree.

VACUUM: Something from which all air has been removed.

VAPOR: The gaseous phase of a substance that is a liquid or a solid at that temperature, for example, water vapor is the gaseous form of water.

VAPORIZE: To change from a liquid to a gas, or vapor.

VENEER: A thin sheet of highly decorative wood that is applied to cheap wood or engineered wood products to improve their appearance and value.

VINYL: Often used as a general name for plastic. Strictly, vinyls are polymers derived from ethylene by removal of one hydrogen atom, for example, PVC, polyvinylchloride.

VISCOSE: A yellow-brown solution made by treating cellulose with alkali solution and carbon disulfide and used to make rayon.

VISCOUS, VISCOSITY: Sticky. Viscosity is a measure of the resistance of a liquid to flow. The higher the viscosity—the more viscous it is—the less easily it will flow.

VITREOUS CHINA: A translucent form of china or porcelain.

VITRIFICATION: To heat until a substance changes into a glassy form and fuses together.

VOLATILE: Readily forms a gas. Some parts of a liquid mixture are often volatile, as is the case for crude oil. This allows them to be separated by distillation.

WATER CYCLE: The continual interchange of water between the oceans, the air, clouds, rain, rivers, ice sheets, soil, and rocks.

WATER VAPOR: The gaseous form of water.

WAVELENGTH: The distance between adjacent crests on a wave. Shorter wavelengths have smaller distances between crests than longer wavelengths.

WAX: Substances of animal, plant, mineral, or synthetic origin that are similar to fats but are less greasy and harder. They form hard films that can be polished.

WEAVING: A way of making a fabric by passing two sets of yarns through one another at right angles to make a kind of tight meshed net with no spaces between the yarns.

WELDING: Technique used for joining metal pieces through intense localized heat. Welding often involves the use of a joining metal such as a rod of steel used to attach steel pieces (arc welding).

WETTING: In adhesive spreading, a term that refers to the complete coverage of an adhesive over a surface.

WETTING AGENT: A substance that is able to cover a surface completely with a film of liquid. It is a substance with a very low surface tension.

WHITE GLASS: Also known as milk glass, it is an opaque white glass that was originally made in Venice and meant to look like porcelain.

WROUGHT IRON: A form of iron that is relatively soft and can be bent without breaking. It contains less than 0.1% carbon.

YARN: A strand of fibers twisted together and used to make textiles.

Set Index